Counter-Cultural Paradigmatic Leadership

Counter-Cultural Paradigmatic Leadership

Ethical Use of Power in Confucian Societies

Gary K. G. Choong

WIPF & STOCK • Eugene, Oregon

COUNTER-CULTURAL PARADIGMATIC LEADERSHIP
Ethical Use of Power in Confucian Societies

Wipf & Stock
An Imprint of Wipf and Stock Publishers
199 W. 8th Ave., Suite 3
Eugene, OR 97401

www.wipfandstock.com

ISBN 13: 978-1-49825-931-6

Manufactured in the U.S.A.

Contents

Foreword

WHY ANOTHER BOOK ON Christian leadership? Because this book directs our attention to some important challenges of leadership when we ponder Jesus' example and teaching. All cultures—whether in the West or the East—are characterized by deep values that promote human flourishing and are compatible with Christianity. Yet all cultures are also characterized by deep values that obstruct human flourishing and are incompatible with Christianity. Our quest is to discern these differences and to bring a distinctly Christian way of living and leading within our respective cultural contexts. As an experienced leader, Dr. Gary Choong offers an insider's view regarding the challenges Christian leaders face within an Asian setting.

Choong provides a helpful study of Confucian ideals in relation to leadership. He identifies the ideal values regarding Paternalistic authority and considers that most of these are compatible with Christianity. Yet the challenge comes in practice, as Choong clarifies. To develop his argument, Choong relies on various sources of knowledge including social science theories on leadership and also biblical studies, particularly emphasizing the life and teachings of Jesus Christ on leadership. What kind of leader are we becoming, is the question that is asked. Choong closes his study with a focus on these key leadership virtues: integrity, humility, and empowerment.

Whether our context is in the East or in the West, I think the book invites us to ponder the question regarding a morally-relevant leadership approach that is both sensitive to culture and to Christian ideals. The book you hold in your hands is a stimulating and challenging reflection from Dr. Choong that provides one such model of integration on this quest to nurture a distinctly Christian practice of leadership.

Klaus Issler
Professor of Christian Education & Theology
PhD in Educational Studies
Talbot School of Theology, Biola University, La Mirada, CA

List of Illustrations

FIGURE

TABLES

Definitions of Terms

character (or moral) formation. A focus on character, whether in philosophical or religious terms, recognizes that personal formation precedes as well as accompanies making good choices. Character not only gives a person a greater capacity to implement a decision but also shapes the kind of decision to be made. It has, therefore, both an informative as well as a performative contribution (Banks and Ledbetter 2004, 97).

Confucianism. Confucianism is a philosophical tradition. It was developed originally in China to deal with social order, veneration of ancestors, and transmitting the wisdom of the past to later ages. . . . Confucianism formalizes the principle of high power distance, which is the essence of its message. Confucian institutions embody a very hierarchical, bureaucratic structure, with a patriarchal expectation of total loyalty and obedience (Carl, Gupta, and Javinda 2004, 523).

Contemporary Confucian Leadership (CCL). [CCL is made up of three elements—][a]uthoritarianism, benevolence, and moral leadership. Authoritarianism refers to a leader's behavior that asserts absolute authority and control over subordinates and demands unquestionable obedience from subordinates. Benevolence means . . . individualized, holistic concern for subordinates' personal and familial well-being. Moral leadership . . . demonstrates personal virtues, self-discipline, and unselfishness (Cheng, Chou, Wu et al. 2004, 91).

ethical (or moral) leadership. [O]ur character and virtues have to match and that we have to *live* what is good and desirable. . . . What we find, then, is that a leader does not have to be a moral hero but has to be a moral person (like everyone else). She should have certain moral qualities that make her a good person and show her integrity (italics author's, Maak and Pless 2006, 43).

ethics. Ethics as incarnational discipleship points to the incarnate Jesus, who taught the Sermon on the Mount and the kingdom of God in the tradition of the prophets of Israel, embodied it in his practices and called us to embody it in our practices of discipleship. This Jesus is our Lord (Stassen and Gushee 2003, 58–59).

Idealized Confucian Leadership (ICL). [It] starts with the foundational beliefs of human goodness and priority for people, which lead to benevolent leadership (ICL). Benevolent leadership has two interrelated components—cultivating oneself to be a sage (or superior) person and leading others as a sage-leader. These lead to the goal of building a harmonious and benevolent world (Yang, Peng, and Lee 2008, 38).

paternalistic authority (PA). Asian cultures have historically had a rich variety of concepts of power. They share, however, the common denominator of idealizing benevolent, paternalistic leadership and of legitimizing dependency.

The foundation of the distinctive form of paternalistic authority common to all Confucian countries was the paramount value of filial piety. Confucian doctrines emphasized that rulers should take the ideal father as their model, and subjects should similarly think of themselves as dutiful children (Pye 1985, vii, 73).

servanthood or servant-leadership (SL). Jesus calls them [the disciples] (and us) to abandon the Gentile exercise of power where everything feeds into one's own comfort, status, authority and position (Matt 23:4–10). Rather, "the greatest among you will be your servant," a servant driven by a humble spirit (Matt 23:11–12). Servant leadership always ends up being other-centered: serving them and building them up.

Leadership and power begin with being the servant of God in the spirit of serving others. The gift of leadership is exercised with a profound humility that reveals a proper respect for God, for oneself and for others (Elmer 2006, 173–4, 178).

Acknowledgments

THIS BOOK IS DEDICATED to the honor and glory of God, whose grace and mercies are new every morning (Ps 90:14).

This book is the result of my doctoral dissertation at Biola University. I have many people to thank. I owe Dr. Klaus Issler a great debt of friendship and love. His wise and scholastic coaching has contributed to my spiritual and intellectual formation. He constantly encourages me to grow my heart for God, and that I will always remember.

I thank Dr. Kevin Lawson, Director, PhD and EdD programs in Educational Studies at Biola University, for his support and recommendation for various scholarships for my study, which made it possible for me to complete the program. The kindness and hospitality that he extended to his students is much appreciated.

Mr. Bob Krauss, librarian at Biola, rendered personal attention and tremendous help to me in accessing resources at Biola and other libraries. More than that, he has demonstrated Christian love, humility, and faithfulness.

I am indebted to three libraries in Singapore for their services—Hon Sui Sen Memorial Library at the National University of Singapore, Trinity Theological College, and Baptist Theological Seminary. The librarians and staff impressed me with their knowledge and excellent service.

I would like to express my thanks to friends at Covenant Community Baptist Church in Singapore who demonstrated God's love in so many ways.

I would like to thank Mr. Michael van Mantgem of Wipf and Stock for his commendable work in editing my manuscript.

I am grateful to my wife for her partnership and support in this project. Thank you, May, for offering much time and careful thought to work alongside me in the writing process.

1

Introduction to the Problem

> Throughout any investigation of leadership is a central thread, the issue of values. The crisis that exists in leadership today is fundamentally a crisis of values. . . . There is no neutral ground from which to examine leadership. The interactive nature of leadership inextricably touches people and their lives, thus calling leadership to a moral plane. . . . Within the issue of values, of course, lie core beliefs and worldviews, which ultimately drive attitudes, motivations, goals, and actions. (Banks and Ledbetter 2004, 33–34)

Kraft defines a worldview as the "culturally structured assumptions, values, and commitments underlying a people's perception of reality" (1989, 20). Values are based on tightly held assumptions about how the world functions and how it should be. Values, attitudes, and behaviors emanate from the worldview that is held as the core within a person.

In East and Southeast Asia, societies such as those that are predominantly Chinese, Japanese, and Korean, are heavily influenced by the philosophy, values, and worldview of Confucius (Bond and Hwang 1986; Hofstede 1980; Pye 1985; Redding 1993).

BACKGROUND OF THE STUDY

Countries that have been under the influence of Confucian culture are predominantly in East and Southeast Asia. Confucianism, which began in China, has influenced the country socially, politically, and culturally for 2,500 years. The impact of Confucian worldview extends beyond

China and continues to influence the political, economic, social, educational, and cultural life of modern day Taiwan, Korea, Japan, Hong Kong, Singapore, and Vietnam.

In his book *Asian Power and Politics* (1985), which focuses on power in East, Southeast, and South Asia, Pye's thesis is "that political power is extraordinarily sensitive to cultural nuances . . . More particularly, Asian cultures have historically had a rich variety of concepts of power. They share, however, the common denominator of idealized benevolent, paternalistic leadership and of legitimizing dependency" (vii). In Confucian Asia, power is seen and understood more in terms of status. Power is also seen as residing in the person and not in the office, and often it is associated with the moral or virtuous character of the individual: "Once power is personalized, legitimacy becomes linked to private behavior; and thus personal morality becomes a public matter" (23). "Paternalism as a general leadership style in Asia reflects the father-like qualities: . . . clear and strong authority, together with concern and considerateness and elements of moral leadership" (Westwood and Chan 1992, 132). Also, "[a]cceptance of authority, deference, loyalty, and an apparent authoritarianism is apparent in most Southeast Asian cultures" (Westwood and Chua 1992, 152). According to Hofstede and Hofstede (2005), people in China, Singapore, Hong Kong, South Korea, Taiwan, and Japan "accept and appreciate inequality but feel that the use of power should be moderated by a sense of obligation" (64).

The culture in Confucian-influenced countries has been classified as collectivistic and high power distance culture (Hofstede 1980; cf. House, Hanges, Javinda et al. 2004). Collectivistic societies integrate their members into cohesive in-groups where the members are provided lifetime protection in exchange for unquestioning loyalty. In high power distance societies, the members are willing to accept social inequality, particularly related to authority and power.

The distinct characteristics of Asian societies under Confucian influence can be summarized as follows. (1) Asian societies are very status conscious, and this has strong behavioral implications for understanding power in relationship leadership: people in lower status will defer to those in higher status; in return the latter must use their status position to benefit those in lower status as a moral obligation. (2) Asian organizations and their understanding of power and leadership are based on "patrimonialism, paternalism, and personalism" (Lowe 2003; Pye 1985;

Redding 1993; Westwood 1997; Putti, Koontz and Weihrich 1998; Rappa and Tan 2003). (3) The ideal model for many Asian organizations is based on familism which depends on the key values of paternalism and dependency (Pye 1985): Power and authority is heavily vested in the male head or patriarch (patrimonial system in family structure), and all decisions made are not to be challenged. (4) Asians, in general, are socialized to show deference, filial piety, and compliance to those in authority (Redding and Wong 1986). (5) While all the above characteristics seem to give the Asian leader a free hand to act in an autocratic manner, the alternative side of the culture demands that there be harmony, be it in the family or in the organization. To maintain harmony, the leader must reciprocate by according subordinates proper respect, concern, care, and consideration in return for the subordinates' compliance and loyalty.

There are two main reasons for my interest in this subject of Confucian paternalistic authority. These two reasons are ultimately related to the main question that I seek to answer in this book: How does a Christian exercise leadership in a Confucian society that promulgates Contemporary Confucian Leadership (CCL)? As a Chinese, I am mindful of my Asian heritage. Born and brought up in Singapore, I was socialized in Confucian values and culture. At the same time, I received my education mainly in the English medium of instruction, and was exposed to Western influence for most of my life. As to matters of ethics, culture, and leadership research in Asia, I am increasingly aware of the good and ills of Confucian influence, especially through the process of writing this book (cf. Chikudate 2004; Koehn and Leung 2004; Tjosvold, Wong, and Hui 2004; Hooker 2003; also the literature base, chapters 3, 5, and 6 of this book).

The first main reason for my interest in this study of Confucian paternalistic authority in leadership is because I have been subordinated to extreme paternalistic authority when I was working in a Christian organization in Singapore. I have struggled long and hard to make sense of Christian leadership in a Confucian paternalistic culture. The clash of values and practices involved (1) biblical submission versus cultural compliance; (2) didactic leadership versus integrity; (3) transactional leadership versus moral transforming leadership; and (4) disempowerment versus shared leadership.

Contemporary (Practiced) Confucian Leadership has been a source of tension in Christian ministry among Asians in Asia as well as

Asian Americans in North America. CCL's values predispose Christian leaders to paternalistic authoritarianism, resembling the nine manifestations of power usage as described in chapter 3. These manifestations of power or authority are also known as coercive and reward power bases in the literature of power and influence theories (cf. discussions in chapter 4). For the purpose of this study, the terms, Contemporary Confucian Leadership, Contemporary (Practiced) Confucian Leadership, Contemporary (Practiced) Confucian Paternalistic Leadership, and Contemporary (Practiced) Confucian Paternalistic Authority will be used interchangeably. The acronym CCL, referring to any of the above, is used for this study.

Second, my interest in this subject of Confucian paternalistic authority in leadership is because I have manifested shades of paternalistic authoritarian leadership in my years of Christian ministry. I was not fully aware of my own blind spots and weaknesses, and I confused these weaknesses as strengths. I have been impatient with people with whom I work in the church and in the theological institution, oftentimes expecting others to do things my way—that fit my agenda and expectations—and focusing on results and performance. In the process, I have run roughshod over associates without giving due consideration to their personal well-being and interests. Positional authority was not accompanied by the virtues of humility, gentleness, patience, and self-control. I have failed to recognize my own dysfunctions and have not surrendered them to the transforming grace of God (cf. Benner 2005, 2004, 2003; Cloud and Townsend 2001, 1995; Coe 2005, 2004, 2000; Hagberg and Guelich 2005; Hands and Fehr 1993; Hoyk and Hersey 2008; Issler 2001; Kets de Vries 2006a; McIntosh and Rima 1997; Seamands 2005; Sledge 1994).

STATEMENT OF THE PROBLEM

Related to the issue of values and worldviews that influence leadership practice, is the subject of ethics or morals. These are related because values and worldviews are central to the domain of morality and ethics. From our value systems we derive principles for actions. After we judge which principles to apply, we "must still *decide* to do the morally right act. Then, finally, we must actually *do* the right act" (Pojman 2002a, 73).

Morality and ethics are two terms that are sometimes used interchangeably. The former is derived from the Latin word *mores*, while the latter comes from the Greek word *ethos*. Both have the idea of "custom." Morals or morality normally refers to customs, precepts, and practices of certain groups of people or cultures. Moral philosophy refers to the theoretical reflection based on morality, and out of these reflections, moral theories are developed, or they may also be known as ethical theories. Hence, as ethics professor Louis S. Pojman (2002a) elaborates, the study of ethics or moral philosophy "seeks to establish principles of right behavior that serve as action guides for individuals and groups. It investigates which values and virtues are paramount to a worthwhile life or society. It builds and scrutinizes arguments in ethical theories and seeks to discover valid principles (e.g., 'Never kill innocent human beings') and the relationship between valid principles (e.g., 'Does saving a life in some situations constitute a valid reason for breaking a promise?')" (2).

Pojman adds that a moral principle shares at least five common traits: prescriptivity, universality, overridingness, publicity, and practicability (7). A moral principle not only shares these five common traits, but it must also be able to be assessed via its actions (right, wrong, obligatory, optional), consequences (good, bad, indifferent), character (virtuous, vicious, neutral), and motive (good will, evil will, neutral).

To assess a moral principle or action, I take reference from ethical theories. Theories that emphasize the nature of the act (right or wrong, such as truth telling) is known as deontological ethics (from the Greek word for "duty"); theories that focus on the consequences in determining moral rightness or wrongness is known as teleological ethics (from the Greek word *telos*, meaning "goal directed"), the most famous of which is utilitarianism; and thirdly, theories that emphasize character or virtue, such as Aristotle's aretaic ethics, or simply known as virtue ethics, because only from good people will flow good or right actions (9–12).

The predominant ethical theory that undergirds Idealized Confucian Leadership is that of virtue ethics. For the idealized Confucian leader, moral character is the highest prized virtue as he leads the people—virtue of love and benevolence (cf. discussion in chapter 2). The underpinnings of the ethical teachings of Jesus Christ in the New Testament (Sermon on the Mount—Matthew 5–7 and Matthew 20:20–28) are virtue ethics and deontological ethics. Taking the teachings of Jesus Christ in the New Testament as a reference point for Christian leaders, this book argues that the basic requirement for Christian leadership is moral character formation, based on virtue and deontological ethics. Rae (2000) argues that deontological ethics, which places emphasis on principles in which actions (or character, or even intentions) are inherently right or wrong, predominate New Testament ethics (28). Rae views virtue ethics as *complementary* to deontological ethics. For the Christian, moral virtues have an intrinsic value in that moral values not only involve the right action, but also the right motive, and attitude. "Virtues are a constitutive element of the good life and especially of being like Christ. Thus, a complementary view of virtues and principles would appear to be more consistent with Scripture. Perhaps virtues are even logically prior to principles, insofar as God's character expresses itself in virtues, and moral rules and principles then are those that are consistent with the outworking of God's virtues" (99–100).

This book also advocates servanthood or Christlike humility (Matt 20:20–28) as the normative pattern for leadership, as evidenced through the teachings and life of Jesus Christ in relation to the exercise of authority.

I have given a brief preview on virtue, deontological, and utilitarian ethical theories as the primary basis to assess the moral foundations and practices of leadership. In this regard, there are three key questions that this book attempts to answer. First, what are the ethical theories that undergird Idealized Confucian Leadership (ICL), Contemporary Confucian Leadership (CCL), and Jesus Christ's teachings (Matt 5:3–12, Matt 20:20–28)? This key question is answered in chapters 2, 3, and 5 respectively. Second, what does social science research in leadership and power-influence theories inform us about leadership, power, and authority—how do they influence moral or ethical leadership practices, and what are their effects on followership? This question is discussed in chapter 4. The third key question, why are moral formation (virtue ethics and deontological ethics) and servanthood (Christlike humility) important as normative practice for Christian leadership in relation to the exercise of authority or power in Confucian culture? I discuss this question in chapter 5. In chapter 6, I summarize my arguments and draw several implications for Christian leaders serving in Confucian societies, and provide suggestions for future research.

IMPORTANCE OF THE STUDY

Contemporary (Practiced) Confucian Paternalistic Authority (a.k.a. CCL) has been a source of tension in Christian ministry among Asians in Asia as well as Asian Americans in North America and Canada. Occurrences of tensions that resulted from Confucian paternalistic authority have been documented in both published and unpublished literature.

Unpublished doctoral level extant literature from a Christian perspective has been written about the subject (e.g., Chelliah 2001 (Singapore); Lee 2004; Oh 2003 (South Korea); Wong 1999 (Canada)). Using quantitative and qualitative research methodologies, these writers have built up cases to argue against the practice of paternalistic authority (PA). They have identified the symptoms and ills of PA in their respective contexts, and have traced the practice of PA to Confucian values and traditions. Their call is a return to New Testament teachings on leadership based on the Apostle Paul and Jesus Christ.

Many of the popular published works have been written with the Asian-American context in view (e.g., Cha, Kang, and Lee 2006; Tokunaga 2003; and Ling 1999). These writers address the heart-breaking issues of paternalistic authority in leadership in Christian ministry. They discuss the critical cultural differences in values, worldviews, and practices between the overseas-born Asians and the American-born Asians that have led to untold conflicts and disagreements in the church and Christian service. Again their plea is to look at the Scriptures for guidance and balance in the exercise of authority and power in Christian leadership.

This book takes the subject of PA a step further beyond the anecdotes and tenets of its practices. By examining the nature of PA in CCL in the light of philosophical moral theories and social studies, its symptoms can be better understood and discerned. A major limitation of PA in CCL is the abuse of power and authority, the corollary of which is the low premium placed on the inherent dignity of followers. When we correlate the practices of CCL with Yukl's (2002) eight criteria for evaluating ethical leadership, more than half of CCL's practices are incompatible with ethical leadership (cf. discussion in chapter 3).

The inadequacies of CCL underscore the need for a more robust ethical or moral foundation for Christian leadership. This book presents a theoretical and practical framework based on Scriptures and aligned with ethical systems. I propose that Jesus Christ's ethical teachings in the SOTM and his teaching and example in Matthew 20:20–28 on the appropriate exercise of power and authority are instructive and normative for Christian leadership. My study demonstrates compatibility between virtue and deontological ethics with these Scriptures.

Another contribution that this book makes is the ethical and moral analyses of PA and Christian leadership. In terms of leadership theories of power and influence, this study subscribes to moral or ethical leadership as seen in the work of James MacGregor Burns, *Transforming Leadership* (1978), and Robert Greenleaf's *Servant Leadership* (1977). Social science research on ethical leadership is compatible with what the Scripture teaches about Christian leadership. These leadership theories complement the biblical and theological argument that virtue and deontological ethics are more robust as complementary ethical systems as opposed to rule-utilitarian ethics. Based on two power-influence theories (and how these theories affect moral leadership practices) and followership responses, I use the framework of French and Raven's power bases (1959); Yukl's eight criteria for ethical leadership (2002); Kelley's style of followership (1992; cf. also Kellerman 2008); and Kanungo and Mendoca's ethical leadership influence process (1996); and analyze CCL's ethical orientations and PA practices (cf. discussions in chapters 3 and 4).

From this study I draw applications for Christian-Asian leaders who serve in a Confucian culture of PA. These applications are relevant to all Christian leaders who serve in cultures that promulgate an authoritarian posture of leadership and followership. These applications are also relevant to secular Asian leaders who are concerned about ethics and morality in the contemporary Confucian culture of paternalistic authority (cf. discussion in chapter 6).

ASSUMPTIONS OF THE STUDY

Discussion in this book is premised upon faith in God, the Ultimate Reality, as revealed in the Person of Jesus Christ in the Holy Scriptures. "The ultimate source for truth, from the perspective of the Christian faith, is embodied in the person of Jesus Christ who claimed to be the truth. Those who seek to be disciples of Jesus are promised access to the truth" (Pazmino 1994, 120).

Culture affects the way a person thinks, feels, and acts. The praxis of leadership is largely influenced by the culture to which one belongs. All human cultures are subject to limitations. Both good and bad elements in leadership can be found in all cultures. There is no one best way or style in the exercise of leadership in any one culture or across cultures. Strengths and weaknesses are inherent in any one or combination of styles of leadership, be it an all-too-directive style (autocratic leadership), or an all-too-participative style (democratic leadership), or any combination in between these two ends of the continuum (cf. Dorfman and Howell, 1997).

Between leaders and followers, variance in terms of levels of morality and subordination can be expected. Willing followership is not necessarily an indicator that the leader is moral (e.g., Kellerman 2004, 2008; Lipman-Blumen 2005; Gangel 2008). The fact that followers accept a certain form of leadership does not mean that that form of leadership is morally beneficial to them. Conversely, unwilling followership is not necessarily errant, such as in the case of a morally upright follower who is unwilling to submit to an unethical or exploitative leader (e.g., Kelman and Hamilton 1989; Conger 1997; Price 2006). Unwilling followership does not necessarily mean that the leader is immoral—there are occasions when a moral leader meets with the defiance of followers (cf. Kellerman 2008; Kelley 1992).

Pojman (2002a) answers a very important question for us: "What is the role of morality in human existence?" He names five important purposes for us to consider: (1) to keep society from falling; (2) to ameliorate human suffering; (3) to promote human flourishing; (4) to resolve conflict of interest in just and orderly ways; and (5) to assign praise and blame, reward and punishment, and guilt (16–18).

Another important question that we need to consider: What is the relationship between morality and religion? The former relies on reason, while the latter relies on revelation; "[b]ut religion can provide added incentive for the moral life, offering the individual a relationship with God, who sees and will judge all our actions" (19).

In this study, I am guided by Christian ethics in the examination of what is right and good and of value, in character and conduct.

> A Christian and theistic position holds that moral principles are objectively meaningful and absolute because they reflect constant moral realities inherent to creation. Persons and cultures sometimes differ in their formulation of fundamental moral norms, or they apply them in different ways in varying situations. But the fact that we do actually communicate on moral issues—disagreeing, persuading one another, and reaching decisions—indicates that there is a reliable cognitive content on moral judgments.

> A striking difference between Christian theism and many other ethical views is that it is committed to a concept of intrinsic goodness. . . . Because humans are the kind of creatures they are—rational, moral, social beings—definite moral considerations are due them. Our created human nature means that we must act and be treated in certain ways. Likewise, if persons must be treated in certain ways, then we are all ethically obliged to treat each other accordingly.
>
> Indeed, performing morally right actions and building morally good character is the fulfillment of a vital aspect of divinely created human nature. . . . To be sure, sin infects the human condition, and any Christian moral philosophy must take this fact into account. (Peterson 2001, 103–5)

SUMMARY

In this first chapter, an overview of the direction of the study is presented. It introduces the reader to the problem, with a preliminary discussion on the subject, of paternalistic authority (PA) as the predominant feature of Contemporary Confucian Leadership (CCL) in Asia. This chapter provides the background to the study, the statement of the problem, importance, and assumptions of the study. The conceptual thrust of chapters 2 to 6 is as follows:

In chapter 2, Idealized (Classical) Confucian Leadership (ICL), traced from the Confucian ideal of sage-kings, and manifested in the idealized virtuous ruler (superior man), upholds high moral values of human relations (virtue and benevolence) and hierarchical relationships to bring about universal peace and harmony in society.

In chapter 3, Contemporary (Practiced) Confucian Leadership or Contemporary Confucian Leadership (CCL), which is predominantly paternalistic-authoritarian with a shade of benevolence and moral obligation, falls short as ethical leadership due to its inclination toward rule-utilitarian ethics.

In chapter 4, based on social science leadership theories and power-influence theories, CCL manifests unethical leadership in its transactional use of positional, coercive, and reward power bases which breeds compliant and uncritical followers as opposed to ethical leadership (based on theories of Burns and Greenleaf) which advocate virtue (character) and deontological (principled) ethics.

In chapter 5, given the prevalence of the practice of CCL among leaders who are in Christian ministry in Confucian societies, the teachings of Jesus Christ on character virtues (in Matt 5:3–12, 17–48) and on servanthood (in Matt 20:20–28) serve as pivotal values in the face of the challenge of CCL practices, particularly in the misuse of power and authority.

In chapter 6, the proposed counter-cultural paradigm for moral leadership is guided by three principles. They are integrity, humility, and empowerment. Implications are drawn from these principles by way of negative examples and direct applications.

2

Idealized Confucian Leadership (ICL): Virtue and Benevolence for Universal Peace and Harmony in Society

ORIGIN AND CONTEXT OF CONFUCIAN POLITICAL IDEAL

CONFUCIUS, ALSO KNOWN AS Master K'ung, or K'ung Fu-Tzu (孔夫子) or Kongzi (551–479 BCE) was born to a poor noble family in the state of Lu, known as Shangtung province today (Mei 1960, 17–35). His family name was K'ung, his personal name Ch'iu. "No other individual in Chinese history has so deeply influenced the life and thought of his people, as a transmitter, teacher, and creative interpreter of the ancient culture and literature, and as a molder of the Chinese mind and character" (17). The era of Confucius was characterized by political decline and social chaos during the Chou (or Zhou 周) dynasty (1122–249 BCE). The nation of China was broken up into many feudal states, constantly warring with one another to secure power and control.

In his lifetime as transmitter and founding father, Confucius set his heart to bring about peace and order in the midst of chaos. Concerned about restoring the social and political order of his day, he urged for "a return to virtue. Unless men individually embraced the ideal of *jen*—humanity, benevolence, or perfect virtue—there was no hope that society could be spared the evil, cruelty, and violence that was destroying it" (18). His political ideal was based on the sage-kings of pre-Confucian era. Sage-kings were men such as Yao and Shun; King T'ang, the wise founder of the Shang dynasty; the great kings, Wen and Wu, of the Chou dynasty; and the Duke of Chou. To Confucius, "[t]hese men embodied the humanity and perfect virtue that he advocated, and their deeds and their reigns represented all that was wise and good in Chinese history and society" (19). "He who exercises government by means of his virtue may be compared to the north polar star, which keeps its place and all the stars turned towards it" (Legge 1930, *The Four Books*: Analects II:1).

IDEALIZED (CLASSICAL) CONFUCIAN LEADERSHIP

The bedrock of Confucian political philosophy is founded upon humane government—"the true king, who rules through moral example" (Chan 1963, 64). The country is based upon a patriarchal foundation, with the family serving as the basis for state rule: "Authority and obedience are necessary to the existence of political order" (Hsu 1932, 35). Hsu adds that "[w]hen the distinction between high and low is made, the existence of propriety (li) and righteousness (yi) is possible. By propriety (li) Confucius means an ethical code enforced by social tradition. . . . By righteousness (yi) Confucius means justice or virtue consisting of benevolent activities that will secure the greatest social harmony" (35).

The Rule of Virtue (德 *)*

The first requirement of benevolent government is the rule of virtue (cf. Hsu 1932, 125–27). Confucius believed that the virtue of the ruler or king was the only way to win the respect of his people and for them to emulate his excellent example. "When a prince's personal conduct is correct, his government is effective without the issuing of orders. If his personal conduct is not correct, he may issue orders, but they will not be followed" (Legge 1930, Analects XIII:6). Confucius developed this thought further: "Let your evinced desires be for what is good, and the people will be good. The relation between superiors and inferiors is like that between the wind and the grass. The grass must bend, when the wind blows across it" (Analects XII:19).

The Rule of Love (Benevolence) (仁 *)*

The second requirement of benevolent government is "the parental love of the ruler for the ruled" (Hsu 1932, 126). The need is for a virtuous emperor or ruler to love the people and look after their welfare: "To rule a country of a thousand chariots, there must be reverent attention to business, and sincerity; economy in expenditure, and love for men; and the employment of the people at the proper seasons" (Legge 1930, Analects I:5). The goal of rulership is to look after the needs of the people, and not to benefit himself, "[t]hus love of the people is the highest ideal of government" (Hsu 1932, 114).

Exercising love calls for the ruler to carefully choose personnel who are able and virtuous to assist him in governing the country. The populace's confidence in the government will only be ensured when upright personnel are appointed to oversee the population: "Advance the upright and set the crooked, then the people will submit. Advance the crooked and set the upright, then the people will not submit" (Legge 1930, Analects II:19).

The concepts of love and virtue appear in both Confucian teachings and the Bible. Love is the cardinal virtue in Jesus' teaching (Matt 22:37–40; 5:43–48); the cardinal virtue in Confucian teaching is love or benevolence (*ren*). Jesus teaches the golden rule (Matt 7:12). Confucius also teaches the golden rule, but states it negatively: "Do not do to others what you do not wish done to yourself" (Analects XII:2; XV:23). However, there are also differences between the two. It goes beyond the scope of this study to examine these similarities and differences. For further study, please consult Chang, 1999; Ching, 1977; Kung and Ching, 1989; and Soon, 1984.

The Theory of the Mandate of Heaven and the Theory of Rebellion

Confucius pointed out four forms of evil that rulers should take note: "cruelty, oppression, injury, and meanness" (Hsu 1932, 126). During the Chou Dynasty (1122-249 BCE) the theory of the Mandate of Heaven (*Tien Ming* 天 明) was developed (Watson 1960, 190). The Chou rulers called this doctrine "the decree of Heaven" (Creel 1953, 15).

According to the theory of the Mandate of Heaven, the ruler was the "Son of Heaven" (*Tien Zi* 天 子). His authority was bestowed upon him from Heaven and he was to be a steward of that trust to look after the welfare of the people that he governed (cf. Legge, *Chinese Classics, vol.* 3, 1960, 421–33; Legge, *The Four Books*, 1930, Analects XX). The ruler was the representative of the people before Heaven. He bore the sole responsibility for any offences the people had committed against Heaven. In times of natural disasters and calamities, considered as divine judgments from above, he would act as the intermediary to offer prayers and sacrifices to Heaven.

However, when a ruler failed to rule his subjects with virtue, he stood to lose the right to rule and another virtuous person might replace him. This is known as the theory of rebellion: "Heaven rejected rulers because, among other crimes, they did not treat the people well. The result was to establish, in theory, the principle that the rulers existed for the sake of the people, rather than the reverse, and that they held their powers only in trust, as a kind of stewardship, subject to revocation if they did not use them well" (Creel 1953, 18).

The authority of the earthly emperor to rule was predicated upon his virtues and love for the people as a steward of Heaven. Confucius approved the right of the people to rebel when the king lost his virtue or became a tyrant. The same sentiment was echoed by Mencius (371–289 BCE), a famous disciple of Confucius: "If a ruler regards his ministers as his hands and feet, then his ministers will regard him as their belly and heart. If a ruler regards his ministers as dogs and horses, the ministers will regard him as any other man. If a ruler regards his ministers as dirt and grass, the ministers will regard him as a bandit and an enemy" (Legge 1930, 733, *The Works of Mencius*, bk. 4, III:1).

What was the ideal society that Confucius had hoped and wished for in his time? Watson (1960) comments: "It [Book of Rites, *Li Jing*] has been traditionally taken as representing Confucius' highest ideal in the social order, the age of Grand Unity (ta-t'ung), in which the world was shared by all the people (t'ien-hsia wei kung)" (191). This Grand Unity would signify a period of wealth, health, peace, justice, and goodwill among humankind.

THE IDEALIZED CONFUCIAN LEADER

For Confucius, the leader must be a superior man (*jun zhi* 君 子), one who exhibits high morals and be an example to society. The virtues of a superior man are benevolence, righteousness, wisdom, trustworthiness, filial piety, and ritual propriety. "According to Confucius, if you know how to cultivate your own character, you will know how to shape others and how to lead the family and the state. The cultivation of one's character is prerequisite for leadership" (Yang, Peng, and Lee 2008, 38).

Education and self-development are means to becoming a superior man. In his discourse with his disciples, Confucius commented that he fell short of the ideal of the superior man: "In letters I am perhaps equal to other men, but the character of the superior man, carrying out in his conduct what he professes, is what I have not attained to" (Legge 1930, Analects XXXII:32).

There are at least seven key traits that distinguish the superior man (De Bary 1991, 20). (1) His manifestations of virtues are in forms that benefit the people (Legge 1930, Analects XV:34; XX:2). (2) His respectful and reverential mannerisms command respect from others (Analects XI:30). (3) His cultivation of rites which is a disciplined practice of social and religious observances of forms and rituals governs his behavior with respect to others (Analects I:19; XII:2; XIII:4; XIV:44). (4) His kind, generous, and respectful behavior toward others in social settings (Analects XVIII:2; XI:24). (5) His trust in relations with the people that he associates with (Analects XII:7; XIII:4; XV:25). (6) His reasonable expectations of others, according to circumstances (Analects XIX:10). (7) His personal desire to grow and learn, and his responsibility toward the education of the people (Analects XI:20; XIII:4; XIII:29). Furthermore, the superior man exercises the Middle Way (*zhong yong*)—moderation in all things in relation to nature and people.

The two virtues of *ren* and *li* are Confucius's most prominent teachings in the Analects (Chan 1963, 1967; Tu 1985; Fung 1952; Yao 2000). When asked about the concept of *ren* (humanity), Confucius replied: "To be able to practice five virtues everywhere in the world constitutes humanity." When pressed further, Confucius explained: "Courtesy, magnanimity, good faith, diligence, and kindness. He who is courteous is not humiliated, he who is magnanimous wins multitude, he who is of good faith is trusted by the people, he who is diligent attains his objective, and he who is kind can get service from the people" (Mei 1960, 28, citing Analects XVII:6).

The Cardinal Virtues of Ren and Li

The word *ren* is made up of two Chinese characters, *ren* (man or human being 人) and *er* (the number "two" 二) (Fung 1952, 69). *Ren* is an ideogram of a human figure, referring to the selfhood of man, and *er* depicts the relationship between two persons. *Ren* has been translated as "goodness," "benevolence," (or "love"), "the supreme excellence in man or perfect virtue" (Mei 1960, 28). Wing-Tsit Chan defines *ren* (or spelled as *jen* by other authors) this way: "Jen means humanity, that is, that which makes a man a moral being. As a particular virtue, it means love" (Chan 1963, 40). *Jen* as the universal virtue embraces other virtues (Ching 1977, 93). Practicing *jen* calls for one to have "the ability from one's own self to draw a parallel for the treatment of others" (Fung 1952, 71, citing Analects VI:28).

According to Confucius, *jen* is the inner and foundational virtue for other outward virtues to be formed and nurtured. Without this inner compass of *jen*, outward virtues would lose their meaning: "When a man is not virtuous [*jen*], of what account are his ceremonial manners [*li*]? (Legge 1930, Analects III:3)." In Confucian thought, *jen* and *zhi* (wisdom or knowledge) are seen as a pair (Legge 1930, cf. Analects IV:2; XI:21; IX:28; XII:22; XIV:30; XV:32).

Confucius considered love as the underpinning of *jen*. When asked by a disciple, Fah Chih, concerning humanity, he replied, "Love men" (Legge 1930, Analects XII:22). Love must begin at home. "Filial piety and fraternal submission!—are they not the root of all benevolent actions?" (Legge 1930, Analects I:2). When asked about the practice of *jen* by his disciple, Confucius answered: "The man of jen is one who, desiring to be established himself, seeks also to establish others; desiring to be enlarged himself, he seeks also to enlarge others; to be able from one's own self to draw a parallel for the treatment of others: that may be called the way to practice jen" (Legge 1930, Analects VI:28).

The practice of *jen* requires the person to first consider the other person and put himself in the position of that other person (Legge 1930, Analects XII:2). This is how *jen* is practiced and such practice is called reciprocity.

"The word *li* (ritual or rite) is expressed in writing by a picture of a ritual vessel. The original meaning is said to be 'arranging ritual vessels'; and this may very well be true, for it appears to be cognate to a number of words meaning 'to arrange in proper order,' to be put in sequence,' etc." (Waley 1938, 64).

Li may be defined as rules of propriety and proper conduct (rites). "Thus the li are imposed on man from the outside. But besides this outer mould, we each still have within us something which we may take as a model for our conduct" (Fung 1952, 72). "Thus the li perform two functions: that of regulating (chih) human emotions; and that of refining (wen) them, that is, giving them a refined expression" (338).

> Of all things by which the people live, the *li* are the greatest. Without them, there would be no means of regulating the services rendered to the spirit of Heaven and Earth; there would be no means of distinguishing the positions of ruler and subject, superior and inferior, old and young; and no means of keeping separate the relations between man and woman, father and son, elder and younger brother, and of conducting the intercourse between contracting families in a marriage, and the frequency (of the reciprocities between friends) or their infrequency. (Fung 1952, 339, citing the Book of Rites, *Li Jing*, XXVIII)

The *li* thus maintains the social gradations of relationships that are necessary in society if there is to be harmony. *Li* serves to structure social behaviors and relationships so as to maintain order in hierarchical structures of relationships and duties. *Li* serves as the outward expression of *ren*. *Ren* and *li* are mutually dependent. Without *ren*, *li* becomes cold formalism; and *ren* needs to be regulated by *li*.

The Five Relationships (Wu Lun)

Confucian values revolve around the social hierarchy of The Five Relationships (*Wu Lun*), which is governed by gender, age, and seniority. "The duties of universal obligations are five, . . . those between sovereign and minister [君 臣], between father and son [父 子], between husband and wife [夫 妇], between elder brother and younger [兄 弟], and those belonging to the intercourse of friends [朋 友]" (Legge 1930, *The Four Books: Doctrine of the Mean*, XX:8). "The Five Relationships have formed the general pattern of Chinese society. It is to be noted that only one of the five is biological, that all are defined in moral terms, and that all are reciprocal" (Chan 1963, 70).

In Confucius' teaching and philosophy, the concept of filial piety (*Xìao* 孝) is the root of all virtues; all other virtues sprout from that root. "With their social organization centered in family and kinship, the Chinese have traditionally held on to filial piety as their cardinal virtue. . . . [A]ll other virtues, from honesty to love of spouse, from devotion to the ruler to interest in abstract principles, were either subordinated to this cardinal virtue or modified by it, defined in terms of it or even eliminated by it" (Hsu 1998, 61).

When asked about the meaning of filial piety, Confucius replied: "That parents, when alive, should be served according to propriety; that when dead, they should be buried according to propriety; and that they should be sacrificed according to propriety" (Legge 1930, Analects II:5).

SUMMARY

Idealized (Classical) Confucian Leadership (ICL), traced from the Confucian ideal of sage-kings and manifested in the idealized virtuous ruler (superior man), upholds high moral values of human relations (virtue and benevolence) and hierarchical relationships to bring about universal peace and harmony in society.

This chapter presented the framework for the understanding of ICL from the perspectives of its historical origin, its two core values, and the concept of the superior man. First, the chapter briefly described the historical origin and context of ICL. The era of Confucius was characterized by political decline and social chaos during the Chou dynasty (1122–249 BCE). Confucius set his heart to bring about peace and order in the midst of chaos.

Second, this chapter presented the source of ICL: The ideal political hierarchy of rulership is based on two important Confucian values (1) the *rule of virtue* and (2) the *rule of love* (benevolence); however, for lack of virtue and benevolence, a despotic ruler will be replaced, according to the mandate of heaven and the theory of rebellion (cf. Wright 1964). I posit that ICL is a leadership philosophy that is based on philosophical virtue ethics in orientation and practice (cf. Yang, Peng, and Lee 2008).

Third, this chapter described the Confucian concept of the superior man (*jun zhi*). The superior man embodies the values of rule of virtue and rule of love. The idealized ruler is a superior man who exhibits high morals and is an example to society through the cultivation of virtues *ren* and *li* , and the practice of the Five Relationships (*Wu Lun*), and of filial piety (*Xi*ào).

This chapter is important to the whole study as it forms the basis for our discussions concerning the exercise of authority or power for the Christian leader in a Confucian society in the present day. It provides the basis specifically in two areas: first, to better understand and evaluate the present-day practices of Confucian leadership and second, to evaluate the values of Confucian leadership against ethical theories (chapter 3), social leadership theories (chapter 4), and teachings of Jesus Christ (chapter 5).

3

Ethical Analysis of Contemporary (Practiced) Confucian Leadership (CCL): Rule-Utilitarian Ethics

THE LEGACY OF CONFUCIAN leadership remains very much a part of those societies that have been historically influenced by Confucian values. However, the present-day practice of Confucian leadership in these societies is a departure from its idealized (classical) form, essentially in its ethical orientation.

CONTEMPORARY (PRACTICED) CONFUCIAN PATERNALISTIC LEADERSHIP (CCL): AUTHORITARIAN, BENEVOLENT, AND MORAL LEADERSHIP

From the literature concerning the practice of Confucian-based paternalistic authority in the Asian context, the use of power or authority has much to do with a "special reverence for status and power" (Kao and Young 1992, 277). Paternalistic authoritarianism as found in the Asian context stems from the Confucian values of filial piety and ancestor worship, reflecting cultural expectations of the son in relation to the father (Farh and Cheng 2000). This power hierarchy is not only found in familial relationships but in organizations as well (cf. also Kets De Vries 1996).

Contemporary (Practiced) Confucian Paternalistic Authority may be labeled authoritarian, benevolent, and moral leadership, with the moral dimension being the weakest of the three. The various facets and key leadership practices or strategies of paternalistic authority is influenced by authoritarianism as primary, benevolence as secondary, and moral as obligatory. Paternalistic authority may be defined as "a style that combines strong discipline and authority with fatherly benevolence and moral integrity couched in a personalistic atmosphere" (Cheng et al. 2004, 91). Three important elements are found in this form of Confucian leadership: "Authoritarianism, benevolence, and moral leadership. Authoritarianism refers to a leader's behavior that asserts absolute authority and control over subordinates and demands unquestionable obedience from subordinates. Benevolence means . . . individualized, holistic concern for subordinates' personal and familial well-being. Moral leadership . . . demonstrates personal virtues, self-discipline, and unselfishness" (Cheng et al. 2004, 91).

Westwood (1997) uses the term paternalistic headship (445), as an alternative term to paternalistic authority in Confucian leadership. He argues that this term is more appropriate as it "emerge[s] out of a traditional, but persisting, cultural ethos that provides a legitimized and workable frame based upon 'natural' authority structures and social injunctions for harmony and reciprocity" (445–46).

This form of Confucian leadership, particularly in business, management, social enterprise, government, and education have been documented in East Asian countries (Farh et al. 2008; Fu et al. 2008; Farh and Cheng 2000; Lowe 2003); Japan and South Korea (Cho 1991; Lee 2001; Oh 2003); Taiwan (Chen 1991; Cheng et al. 2004; Silin 1976; Yan and Hunt 2005); Southeast Asian countries (Carl, Gupta, and Javinda 2004; Pye 1985; Silverthorne 2005; Westwood and Chan 1992; Westwood and Chua 1992); Hong Kong (Cheung and Chan 2005; Lam 2002; Redding and Wong 1986; Westwood 1997); and Singapore (Bell 1997; Ji, Ngin, and Teo 2008; Low 2006; Sheh 2003).

Academic textbooks written from an Asian or Southeast Asian perspective acknowledge the significant influence of Confucian values in management and leadership theories and practices (e.g., Farh et al. 2008; Farh and Cheng 2000; Cha 1993; Clegg, Dunphy, and Redding 1986; Putti 1991; Putti, Koontz, and Weihrich 1998; Westwood 1992).

Various published journal research and studies have also validated the significant influence of Confucian values in Confucian societies leading to the exercise of paternalistic authority. Confucian values have influenced the manner in which leaders, businessmen, educators, and politicians operate in the realm of businesses, politics, education, human resource, and society as a whole.

KEY PRIMARY LITERATURE REVIEW OF CCL (PATERNALISTIC AUTHORITY)

This section gives a literature review on the subject of paternalistic authority. The key works are discussed as follows.

Redding (1993)

Using Weber's (1947) three seminal ideas on authority, namely, traditional, charismatic, and rational-legal, Redding (1993) classifies paternalism under the broad cultural and historical context of patrimonialism, "the distinguishing feature of which is that the ultimate power, which rests with the head of state, is personal and is dispensed and dispersed by representatives who also interpret it personally" (59). Four characteristics of patrimonialism are inherent in Confucian cultures: paternalistic ethos, clear hierarchy, reciprocal vertical obligation, and power-ownership (144).

Based on the findings of Robert Silin (1976), Lucian Pye (1985), and Frederick Deyo (1978, 1983), Redding summarizes seven distinct features on paternalistic authority: (1) dependence of the subordinate, (2) personalized loyalty of the subordinate leading to conformity, (3) sensitized authoritarianism to subordinates' views, (4) authority rests upon a person, (5) aloofness and distancing within the hierarchy, (6) ambivalent and unclear intentions of the leader, and (7) the leader as exemplar and "teacher" (Redding, 130).

Redding studied the economic culture of overseas Chinese in Hong Kong, Taiwan, and the Southeast Asian countries of Singapore, Indonesia, the Philippines, Malaysia, and Thailand. He suggests three lasting psycho-social legacies of Confucian China. These are (1) insecurity which stems from their past experience of a society that did not guarantee them a system of property rights, and lack of trust outside delimited groups; (2) the Confucian heritage of paternalism leading to familism and authoritarianism, which creates a deep sense of dependence and acceptance of hierarchy; and (3) personalism which denies the flourishing of objectivity and neutrality, and hence no true rational and professional bureaucracy can sprout (117).

Silin (1976)

In his study of unipowered organizations (i.e., large private firms controlled by single individuals) in Taiwan, Silin relates organizational and management behaviors to their cultural values. He notes that Taiwanese are heavily influenced by Confucian social and political values: "Considerable formalism exists in all authority relationships. Any attempts at creating a more informal, affective atmosphere on the part of subordinates are interpreted by leaders as efforts to transform authority relationships into those of equality or friendship, thereby undercutting the leader's prerogatives. Leaders suppress these inclinations on the part of subordinates" (128–29).

Westwood and Chan (1992), Westwood (1997)

In their academic and insightful study of Confucian paternalistic authority, Westwood and Chan describe eight facets of paternalistic style of leadership. These eight facets are briefly described below.

Dependence Orientation of Subordinates

Due to the benevolent paternalistic nature of leadership in Confucian culture, subordinates feel that those in authority are obliged to take care of them and they develop an attitude of dependence, while at the same time responding with compliance to those in authority. "Most Asians feel they will be accepted and looked after by the collectivity if they behave in the expected ways. The ideal position for the individual in his relationships with authority is much like the situation a child might wish to have within the family" (Pye, 328).

Personalism

"Loyalties are to the person, not the system or other abstractions. . . . [T]he defining characteristic of personalism is the tendency to allow personal criteria and relationships to enter into decision making and action" (Westwood and Chan, 134–35). Since the leader is the center of everything, he is in a position to dispense fear or favor depending on the circumstances.

Relational personalism necessitates for a clear distinction between in-group members or insiders (*zijiren*) and out-group members or outsiders (*wairen*). When it comes to resource allocation, there are three distinct groups of people according to Gabrenya and Hwang (1996): expressive (familial), mixed (friends), and instrumental (strangers). Yang (1995) made similar distinctions: family (*jia*), insiders (*shu*, meaning "cooked"), and outsiders (*sheng*, meaning "raw"). Hence, in the practice of *ren* (benevolence), there is a hierarchy of love based on the degree of intimacy of the relationship (Gabrenya and Hwang 1996, 311). Personalism defines the nature of loyalty from subordinates as well as how others are perceived by the leader.

Related to personalism is the concept of *Guanxi* (关 系). This concept may be defined as "the granting of favours either directly on the basis of personal relationships or to others to whom one has a special interpersonal linkage" (Smith and Zhong, 329).

Bond and Hwang (1986) summarize the essential aspects of Confucianism in Chinese social psychology as follows: "A person exists through, and hence is defined by, his relationships with others; these relationships are structured in a hierarchical order and form; social order is maintained by each person's honoring the other person through the requirements as set and defined in that role relationship in society" (216).

Moral [Obligatory] Leadership

Moral leadership for the Confucian means a sacred responsibility and obligation to look after the welfare of their subordinates. The Confucian leader needs to be seen as moral, "[n]ot 'moral' in the sense of conformance to high or universal principles, but rather of behaving within situations and relationships in culturally required and expected ways" (Westwood 1997, 467). In other words, the Confucian leader needs to show reciprocation (moral obligation) of subordinate's compliance and loyalty with "considerateness, human heartedness and a recognition of their personhood" (Westwood, 467). Sheh (2003) puts it this way: "[T]he Chinese leader has a moral responsibility and obligation to look after the welfare and well-being of the employees" (151).

Harmony Building

One of the key goals in Confucian leadership is harmony. "Authoritarian aspects of the style can only be sustained in an environment of harmoniousness. At the same time, the conditions that create the possibility for order and compliance—natural hierarchy, mutual dependence and obligation, respect for authority, and high Power Distance—also create a naturally harmonious social pattern" (Westwood and Chan, 135).

Conflict Diffusion

A key feature in Confucian culture is the avoidance or minimization of conflict in all forms of relationships. "Asian cultures are often described as conflict avoiding. . . . Asian cultures have few mechanisms for resolving conflict once it has developed but many mechanisms for preventing it from emerging" (135–36). Leung (1996), in his study on "The role of beliefs in Chinese culture," purports that in a collectivist society like the Confucian Chinese society, "it is widely believed that it is more effective to resolve disputes through negotiation and compromise rather than confrontation" (258). Leung goes on to report that employees in Hong Kong, when surveyed, ranked compromise first and competition last when faced with conflicts.

Aloofness and Social Distance

The paternalistic leader often acts with an air of aloofness and keeps a distance between himself and his subordinates. "Despite the personalism of Asian leadership, heads/leaders tend to keep a social distance from subordinates and to remain somewhat aloof. This is partly the result of authoritarianism" (136).

Didactic Leadership

The paternalistic leader employs didactic leadership. This means that the leader understands the power of information and resources, and hence he adopts a highly selective manner in the dispensing of information and resources in order to protect his dominance. Using the concept propounded by Silin (1976), didactic leadership refers to: "The leader's possession and strategic use of information, knowledge, and expertise as a resource. He will play the role of master and will selectively, and in fragmented manner, pass information and knowledge on to the subordinates. No individual will be given access to all that the leader has. This obviously builds up and sustains that dependence of the subordinates and bolsters the power of the leader" (Westwood and Chua, 136).

Dialogue Ideal

In his relationships with subordinates, the leader in Confucian culture adopts face-saving postures to maintain order and propriety in the relationship. "[The leader] must respect the dignity and 'face' of subordinates. The superior-subordinate relationship is not, then, seen as antagonistic, rather as a natural hierarchy. A dialogue between the leader and the led is maintained through which the leader remains aware of the sentiments and views of subordinates, and subordinates are able to sense the expectations and intentions of superiors" (Westwood and Chan, 136–37).

There are six forms of face and shame (脸, 羞) behaviors as researched by Bond and Hwang (1986): enhancing one's own face, enhancing the other person's face, losing one's own face, hurting the other's face, saving one's own face, and saving the other's face (246–49).

There are three important strands to understanding Chinese or Confucian social interactions: face (*mianzi*), favor (*renqing*), and networking (*guanxi*). Gabrenya and Hwang (1996, 312–13) cited the work of H. C. Hu (1944) that distinguishes between *lian* and *mianzi* in Chinese society. The former (*bu yao lian*, meaning "doesn't want face") refers to a person's character being slurred, and notions of shamelessness or immorality are attached to the concept. The latter (*mei you mianzi*, meaning "has no face") refers to a person's loss of honor and glory in the eyes of a community. Hence: "An individual's *lian* (or *mianzi*) can be preserved by faithful compliance with ritual or social norms" (312).

To understand the exercise of power in Asia, Pye (1985) asserts that "it is necessary to look through the formal arrangements of authority to the dynamics of the informal relationships . . . which usually are highly personalized, and make up the substance of real power in the society" (285).

Farh and Cheng (2000)

In their "[c]ultural analysis of paternalistic leadership in Chinese organizations" among overseas Chinese family businesses, Farh and Cheng trace their deep cultural roots of the three dominant elements (to varying degrees) in paternalistic leadership (PL) of the Chinese: authoritarianism, benevolence, and morality. There are three key elements of contemporary paternalistic authority, and their corresponding follower-responses as depicted in table 3.1, p. 30.

The authors lay down three corresponding assumptions to authoritarian, benevolent, and moral aspects of paternalistic authority: subordinates must have been socialized to be dependent, compliant, and accept vertical hierarchy; subordinates must engender the feeling of indebtedness to their superiors; and subordinates must be able to identify and replicate the moral behavior of their superiors. Harmony results when the subordinate reciprocates correspondingly to the superior's stance toward whichever of the three varying elements of paternalistic leadership (97). "In this sense, PL is based more on followership than on leadership" (99).

Farh and Cheng explain the cultural roots of authoritarianism, benevolence, and morals in paternalistic authority: Deep strong belief in the five cardinal relationships in Confucian socialism, particularly the three bonds (father-son, husband-wife, and brother-brother) defines the social order in Chinese society. The father-son relationship, filial piety, is the most important of all societal relationships—literally referring to the "submission to the will of the father"—"filial piety is not just a defining virtue for a perfect man, but the glue that holds the patriarchal family together and the cornerstone of an orderly Confucian society" (101). This social hierarchy was politicized and practiced throughout the imperial dynastic rules in China's historical development with the last dynasty, the Qing (1644–1911), maintaining "the most authoritarian rule." Farh and Cheng continue: "The non-reciprocal obligations owed by inferiors to superiors within this framework set the authoritarian tone of much of life in traditional China until the end of imperial times" (103). Patriarchalism is handed down to modern day Chinese family businesses in the form of pan-familism whereby "it is natural for the Chinese to treat the family as a prototype for almost all other organizations" (103–4). The owner or supervisor takes on the role of the father, while the subordinate the role of the son: "[T]he all-powerful boss dictates, and the subordinate listens and complies" (104).

In the Confucian ideal society, dyadic role relationships are based on mutuality—those who assume roles of superiority, as in fathers, elders, etc., have obligations to treat their subordinates, as in sons and juniors, etc., with gentleness, kindness, benevolence, and righteousness. Subordinates should reciprocate by showing filial duties, obedience, submission, loyalty, conformance, and deference to their superiors. This dyadic mutuality between superior and subordinate forms the cultural mandate and expectations of leader benevolence and follower obedience. Farh and Cheng highlight that this dyadic mutuality is not always symmetrical—"[t]he tradition of the Three Bond has made it clear that even when superiors behave in contradiction to their role requirements, inferiors are still expected to fulfill their role obligations" (104).

In today's business and social contexts, Farh and Cheng argue that fatherly benevolence expressed today is based on the simple concept of *bao* (gratitude). *Bao* has the idea of reciprocity—as one is treated well, one is expected to reciprocate (*bao*) in kind. The employee is expected, out of indebtedness, to repay (or to reciprocate) to the superior what he or she has received, whether in the form of genuine gratitude, personal obedience to, and compliance to the employer's request, leading to a "patron-client" relationship (105–6).

Confucius advocated cultivation of morals and virtues when governing the people. The most effective form of government was through moral principles, moral examples, and moral persuasion—"the basic requirements for a leader were to demonstrate superior morality by performing the rites associated with his roles" (107).

Farh, Liang, Chou, and Cheng (2008)

Farh, Liang, Chou, and Cheng present a progress update (2008) on Farh and Cheng's previous proposed research (2000) about paternalistic authority and leadership in overseas Chinese family businesses. The main thrust of this updated research (2008) is their modification to their previous model of PA with regard to the three key elements of Confucian leadership: authoritarian, benevolent, and moral. These three elements of contemporary Confucian leadership are used to define eight leadership types through the grid of Fiedler's contingency theory in leadership (1967). Farh et al. dichotomize the three elements of CCL and cross these as HA vs. LA (High Authoritarianism vs. Low Authoritarianism), HB vs. LB (High Benevolence vs. Low Benevolence), and HM vs. LM (High Moral character vs. Low Moral character) (184–86). The revised contingency model proposes involving these eight types of paternalistic authority in CCL. This is an average leadership style model of leadership in which authoritarian leadership leads to compliance by subordinates, benevolent leadership leads to reciprocal obligation, and moral leadership leads to respect and identification with the leader. As expected, the respondents give high ratings to the positive types of CCL, and conversely, they give low ratings to the negative types of CCL. In between the spectrum, there are different combinations of high and low ratings given by different respondents as followers. It is interesting to note that "[i]n selecting ideal leaders, employees eschewed PL [paternalistic leadership] types with low moral character, regardless of the leader's benevolence and authoritarianism. . . . [this] suggest[s] that moral character is a necessary condition for emerging leaders in Chinese organizations" (191). The authors go on to add: "In a culture with high power distance and high particularism, such as China, followers tend to depend on the leaders . . . Without self imposed moral restraints by the leader, authoritarian and benevolent leadership styles could easily slip into manipulative tactics that serve only the goals of the leader at the expense of the followers" (191).

The dynamics of the three strands of paternalistic authority in Contemporary (Practiced) Confucian Leadership is given in table 3.1. The table is synthesized from various literature dealing with contemporary Confucian paternalistic authority practiced among Chinese leaders in business, management, and education. The three varying stances of Contemporary Confucian Paternalistic Authority are gleaned from the extant literature review base (Farh and Cheng 2000; Lowe 2003; Pye 1985; Redding 1993; Silin 1976; Westwood 1997; Westwood and Chan 1992; Westwood and Chua 1992).

TABLE 3.1. Contemporary (Practiced) Confucian Leadership: Authoritarian, Benevolent, and Moral leadership (adapted from tables in Westwood 1997, 453, Westwood and Chan 1992, 125; and Farh and Cheng 2000, 98, 108)

Three varying stances of CCL	Leadership practices and strategies	Cultural roots: Confucian values	Followership-response
Authoritarian stance	High control, low trust: Underestimation of subordinate competence Reputation building Didactic leading Aloofness and distancing Ambivalent stance Protection of dominance Abuse and misuse of power and authority Corruption Patronage and nepotism Cronyism	Political values of hierarchy: Five relationships and three bonds Three-thousand-year history of imperial rule Centralized imperial power and authority Law and punishment Legalism	Compliance: Obey authority Conformance Dependence Loyalty Harmony Respect and fear Face and shame

Three varying stances of CCL	Leadership practices and strategies	Cultural roots: Confucian values	Followership-response
Benevolent stance	Paternalistic individualized care: Familial treatment Job security Protection of subordinates	Rule of benevolence: Obligation of the father and emperor (patriarchy/familism) Human heartedness and propriety (*ren* and *li*)	Gratitude: Reciprocity Beholden Face and shame
Moral stance	Moral obligation: Unselfishness Lead by example Does not abuse authority Separation of personal and corporate interest	Rule of virtue: Political hierarchy of rulership under the mandate of heaven	Identification: Identify with leader's moral behavior Imitate moral behavior

The leadership practices and strategies and followership-response are a composite summary of various authors and researchers, namely from significant research of Silin, Redding, Westwood and Chan, Westwood and Chua, Pye, Lowe, Farh and Cheng. The cultural roots of Confucian values, philosophy, and practices are located in many sources (e.g., De Bary 1989a, De Bary 1989b; Bond 1996; Chan 1963, 1967; Farh and Cheng 2000; Gabrenya and Hwang 1996; Hofstede 1980; Hsieh 1967; F. Hsu 1971, 1998; L. Hsu 1932; Legge 1930; Lowe 2003; Mei 1960; Moore 1967; Pye 1985; Redding 1993; Westwood 1997; Westwood and Chan 1992; Westwood and Chua 1992; Wu 1987; Yao 2000).

Westwood and Chan (1992, 118–43) discuss the difference between leadership (Western model: "accorded by the followers to the leader," 123) and headship (Asian model: "being imposed on the followers," 123). The Southeast Asian perspective on headship/leadership based on hierarchy and authority leads to compliance, and patriarchy and filial piety leads to order or harmony. Westwood and Chan highlight the importance of culture to better understand headship in Southeast Asia: "Asian cultures are collectivist and relationship-centred. . . . Throughout Asia, then, heads/leaders are able to assume an authoritarian style and to expect and receive compliance, obedience, loyalty, and deference from subordinates" (130).

One outcome of Confucian paternalistic authority is compliance. Compliance is premised upon two key characteristics of Confucian values: acceptance of hierarchical authority and dependence (Hofstede 1980, 2001). The other outcome is harmony. Harmony is attained through exercising reciprocity of the foundational Confucian values, *ren* (仁) and *li* (礼) in relationships (De Bary 1989a).

Compliance is realized through the exercise of propriety under the "Five Cardinal Rules of Relationships" (*Wu Lun* 五 伦) in hierarchical interpersonal relationships: ruler and subject, father and son, husband and wife, elder brother and younger, and between friends. "It has often been suggested that the Asian management style is authoritarian. This is only half correct. The authoritarian power of the Asian leader is constrained by the need for harmony and by cultural pressures for considerate and proper behavior" (Westwood and Chan, 127). "The apparent absolute power is constrained by the morality of compassion and righteousness. It is such behaviour that is the main source of legitimacy for authoritarian leadership" (Westwood and Chan, 128). Concerning morality, Farh and Cheng (2000) made the observation about the contemporary Confucian paternalistic authority that claims "[t]here is quite a consensus among these writers (i.e., Silin, Redding, and Westwood and Chan) about what constitutes authoritarian and benevolent leader behaviours. Less can be said about moral leadership, since these writers were not consistent on the exact virtues or qualities that a leader must possess in order to be morally superior" (94).

Farh and Cheng (2000), therefore, drew from other studies (Cheng and Zhuang 1981; Ling, Chen, and Wang 1987; Xu 1989; Ling 1991) that point to the importance of a leader's moral character in Chinese organizations. One of these studies (Cheng and Zhuang, 1981) examines effective leadership styles in Taiwanese military personnel. The results showed that most military personnel think moral character as important. The other studies (Ling, Chen, and Wang 1987; Xu 1989; Ling 1991) were conducted in the Peoples' Republic of China. The results showed that a leader's moral character was an important facet of Chinese leadership. These studies suggest that "although leader morality and integrity entail many virtues, two seem to stand out in Chinese contexts: not acting selfishly (especially refraining from abusing authority for personal gain) and leading by example" (Farh and Cheng, 97).

Moral leadership for the Confucian means a sacred responsibility and obligation to look after the welfare of their subordinates. The Confucian leader needs to be seen as moral, "[n]ot 'moral' in the sense of conformance to high or universal principles, but rather of behaving within situations and relationships in culturally required and expected ways" (Westwood 1997, 467). In other words, the Confucian leader needs to show reciprocation (moral obligation) of subordinate's compliance and loyalty with "considerateness, human heartedness and a recognition of their personhood" (467). The Confucian leader is expected to demonstrate a high sense of morals in terms of his mannerisms and behavior. "[T]he Southeast Asian leader . . . needs to be seen to possess valued virtues such as humanity, integrity, compassion, and humility. He needs to behave in ways that conform to the norms of propriety" (Westwood and Chan, 135). Sheh (2003) puts it this way: "[T]he Chinese leader has a moral responsibility and obligation to look after the welfare and well-being of the employees" (151).

Farh and Cheng (2000) put forth two key elements of moral leadership in contemporary Chinese societies based on previous studies (citing Ling, Chen, and Wang 1987; Xu 1989; Ling 1991) conducted in the People's Republic of China and Taiwan. First, leaders do not act selfishly—they do not abuse their authority for personal gain, they refrain from mixing personal interest with that of the business, and they put collective interest ahead of their own. Second, leaders lead by example both at work and in personal conduct (95–98, 116).

Fernandez (2004)

Fernandez proposes an ideal Confucian model of the "Way of the Gentleman . . . [as] being defined as the one who shows in superior behavior the true reflection of his or her character" (23). This ideal person has two aims: (1) self-cultivation toward individual perfection through careful thinking, speaking, and acting and (2) demonstrating exemplary conduct to achieve social harmony (23–25) This ideal leader has two prominent Confucian values, namely kindness (loving people) and justice (treating things properly). From the practice of these two values "we obtain trust and social harmony" (27–28).

Cheung and Chan (2005)

Citing J. Ren (1999), *Ethocratic Study: From the Perspective of Early Confucianism*, Cheung and Chan classify the Confucian style of leadership as one of ruling by ethical values, which emphasize the leader's moral practices, with benevolence being the chief characteristic. In Cheung and Chan's qualitative study of five eminent Chinese CEOs in Hong Kong, who are "best known in business related to trading, insurance, banking, land development, and telecommunication" (51), benevolence, learning, and harmony were the three most common themes in their interviews.

Wong (1998)

Based heavily on Chan's work (1963), K. C. Wong, in his essay "Culture and Moral Leadership in Education" (1998), purports that there are three key elements of moral leadership in Confucian culture. The three elements are an emphasis on ethical humanism which places an "emphasis on people and activities in the world" (119); on learning, "Confucius laid great emphasis on learning" (120); and on moral aspects of learning, "Despite his pragmatism, in Confucius' eyes learning does not primarily serve a vocational purpose. Its function lies in character training" (120).

Fu, Wu, Ye, and Yang (2008)

This brief research on Chinese culture and leadership is limited by the small sample size (focus group) which was collected in Shanghai. The authors use the Chinese Global Leadership and Organizational Behavior (GLOBE) data (cf. House et al. 2004) as their empirical support to briefly introduce the societal culture in China—Confucianism forms the roots—"the virtue of obedience is the cultural root of paternalistic leadership," alluding to the same common Confucian feature as found in Farh and Cheng's research (2000) among many overseas Chinese enterprises (879).

To the question, "what are the qualities of your ideal leader?"—"honesty, trustworthiness, and integrity" are highly prized: "Interviewees unanimously agreed without a high level of integrity no leader can hope to establish high level of credibility, and without credibility no leader can hope to be effective" (896). Even though the Shanghai interviewees view autocratic, self-centered, malevolent, and self-protective leadership as "clear inhibitors of outstanding leadership" (901), the results of GLOBE leadership survey (901) indicate otherwise—it "is comparatively high within the 61 GLOBE countries" (902). The authors confirm that "leadership in China is still somewhat paternalistic," even though leaders are no longer explicitly "heads of families"—"expectations for fatherly roles are still visible" (903).

Ji, Ngin, and Teo (2008)

"The cultural heritage of Singapore reflects values of both the East and the West" (950) and hence provide strong influence on the country's culture and leadership style. The management practices among traditional Chinese companies in Singapore "could best be characterized as paternalistic autocratic. . . . [Employers] made decisions promptly, ordered their subordinates to take certain actions (without sufficiently explaining the rationale behind those actions), and expected their subordinates to comply regardless of the correctness of those actions" (959). Between 1994 to 1997, the authors conducted four focus group interviews with middle managers from the banking and food industries to ascertain the "cultural values and preferred leadership style among managers and leaders" (960).

To the question, "what are the qualities of an outstanding leader?" the interviewees cited "visionary" and "making unpopular but farsighted decisions, and overcoming great difficulties to achieve success" (960). The authors noted something interesting when they observed "that none of the participants, in spite of their ethnic Chinese background, discussed the moral quality of the leaders. Confucian philosophy stresses the moral quality of a leader. If these Chinese participants are heavily influenced by Confucianism, they should have more or less discussed the moral quality of the leaders in the interviews. The fact that moral quality was not even mentioned seems to suggest that the Singapore middle managers are less influenced by traditional Chinese values, such as those from Confucianism" (960–61).

The literature review above demonstrates that Contemporary Confucian Leadership (CCL) may be labeled as paternalistic-authoritarian leadership accompanied with benevolence and moral obligation. I discuss CCL with its three leadership elements: authoritarianism, benevolence, and moral character. These are three key elements under the broad contemporary Confucian leadership style known as paternalistic authority (PA). The literature base demonstrates that contemporary exercise of PA is prevalent in societies that have been heavily influenced by Confucian values.

In the next section of this chapter, I highlight several facets of PA and their entailing leadership practices or strategies in CCL. These facets and strategies are characteristics of the authoritarian, benevolent, and moral posture of the Confucian leader, with authoritarian leadership as the predominant feature. These practices expose CCL's weakest link: the moral element of PA.

THE AUTHORITARIAN POSTURE—NINE STRATEGIES OF PATERNALISTIC AUTHORITY

Westwood and Chua (1992, 163–66) identified at least nine common manifestations of paternalistic authority and its use of positional (status) power (cf. also Farh and Cheng 2000; Lowe 2003; Silin 1976; Redding 1993). They are as follows:

Centralization

All key decisions are held in the hands of the person at the top of the hierarchy and an inner group. This is seen as legitimate power belonging to the head as patriarch. Bond (1996) surmises that decisions reached are not subject to the scrutiny of anyone outside the inner circle, nor the rules, the methods, or the criteria of reaching those decisions (cf. Silin 1976, 63).

Non-Specific Intentions

Paternalistic leaders do not openly declare their intentions to their subordinates. Subordinates must intuit the mind of their superior in order to act appropriately and correctly (Redding and Wong 1986; Silin 1976, 75). This leads to a deep sense of dependence of the followers on their leader for direction and course of action.

Secrecy

This form of "didactic leadership" (Silin 1976) marks the paternalistic leader, who keeps close to his or her heart the plans, intentions, ideas, and other information not made for public consumption. The control of information is held in the hands of the leader and the inner circle where it is only shared selectively. Information is withheld because of self-preservation and because of low trust.

Avoidance of Formality

This mode of operation of leadership avoids the need for accountability, and hence protects the leader from being challenged or questioned. The lack of formalization keeps information and actions obscure from public scrutiny and hence limit the possibility of challenge.

Protection of Dominance

Redding (1993) documents the lack of trust outside the family circle in Chinese enterprises. All power is kept within the family line and the orientation is toward family preservation rather than the organization's progress. In Silin's research (1976), the leader is found to be one who guards his dominance and territorial rights. Silin lists the kinds of tactics used to self-preserve the position of dominance, such as, downplaying the contributions of subordinates (and the expertise that they bring), not welcoming any feedback or constructive criticism, manipulating the subordinates to have a feeling of high dependence on the leader via personalism, creating little team unity among the subordinates, and maintaining loose responsibilities and subjective evaluations that cause them to be at the mercy and will of their leader.

Patronage and Nepotism

Pye (1985) documented patronage and nepotism as two widely accepted uses of power in the Asian context. The personalism and the father-like role of the leader cultivates a culture of dependence and patronage from which the leader provides privileges and security to favored and selected subordinates, which ingratiates them to the leader in a spider web of gratitude and reciprocation. In many cases the actions of such power wielding leaders result in the abuse of power and widespread corruptions in Asia. In the exercise of nepotism and cronyism, those with power will appoint and give opportunities to family members and close associates rather than those whose ties are weaker with the leader (cf. discussion in chapter 6). This ensures that power, positions, and status remain within trusted and loyal members to perpetuate the cycle of control and dominance (cf. Backman 2001).

Non-emotional Ties and Social Distance

Paternalistic leaders adopt this stance (non-emotional ties and social distance) to protect themselves from having to respond to their subordinates' requests and appeals. Such a stance also creates a veneer of mystique and charisma for the leader (cf. Redding 1993).

Cliques and Political Manipulation

Such tactics are used to preserve and strengthen the leader's future. They employ divide-and-conquer tactics to strengthen their position and status in the eyes of subordinates as well as competitors. Secrecy, control of information, personalism, and lack of formality lead to high dependence of employees and subordinates as the leader exercises differential relationships and privileges with everyone. There is no clarity of ethics and values in the relationships. Everything hinges on the leader to form illusions of alliances and cliques, and subordinates have to figure out how to relate to the leader and be rewarded in return for compliance and dependence.

Reputation Building and Networking

Paternalistic leaders are conscious of reputation and status and position. They have to build a perception of high power distance and the higher the distance, the stronger they become. These leaders build their reputation by all means and ways in order that others may perceive them as powerful and this leads to greater dependence and compliance on the part of their followers.

The authoritarian posture of CCL is reflected in what Westwood and Chua refer to as the nine strategies of paternalistic authority. The nine strategies are centralization, non-specific intentions, secrecy, avoidance of formality, protection of dominance, patronage and nepotism, non-emotional ties and social distance, cliques and political manipulation, and reputation building and networking (163–66).

In the following sections, I focus on the ethical deficiencies in the values and practices of CCL. The methodology is to analyze CCL based on (1) philosophical ethical theories and (2) Yukl's eight criteria for ethical leadership. From the discussion on the three ethical theories of virtue, deontology, and utilitarianism, I show that CCL operates mainly along the lines of rule-utilitarian ethics. Further, I argue that CCL, embodied in the nine strategies of contemporary Confucian paternalistic leadership, is found wanting when correlated with Yukl's eight criteria of ethical leadership.

ETHICAL THEORIES OF VIRTUE, DEONTOLOGY, AND UTILITARIANISM

Northouse (2004) posits that ethics is of utmost importance to leadership "because of the nature of the process of influence, the need to engage followers to accomplish mutual goals, and the impact leaders have on establishing the organization's values" (307). Northouse lists five principles for ethical leadership practices that are based on Aristotelian ethics. According to him, (1) ethical leaders respect others; (2) they serve others above themselves; (3) they act justly; (4) they exhibit honesty; and (5) they build community (310–16).

Ethics is generally traced to the Greek word *ethikos*, which means to follow a custom, and *ethos*, which refers to character. *Morality* comes from the Latin word *mores*, which refers to character, or custom, or habit. The etymology of *ethics* connote a person's character, what it means to be a "good person," and the "social rules that govern and limit our conduct, especially the ultimate rules concerning right and wrong, which we call *morality*" (Shaw and Barry 1992, 3). The study of ethics is a study of morality, or the principles of right and wrong. In leadership parlance, both terms ethics and morality are used interchangeably (Rhode 2006, 4).

Virtue Ethics

Virtue ethics emerged in the 1950s as an ethical model to the understanding of practicing the good life (MacIntyre 1981). Virtue is defined as behavior that is shaped and harnessed by moral judgment and discipline as opposed to moral rules, principles, obligations, and consequences. "Virtue ethics seeks to produce excellent persons, who act well out of spontaneous goodness and serve as examples to inspire others" (Pojman 2000, 368). Northouse (2004) defines ethics as "the kind of values and morals an individual or society finds desirable or appropriate . . . and in regard to leadership, ethics has to do with what leaders do and who leaders are" (302).

There are three major spheres of ethical theories: deontological ethics which is based on duty or rule; teleological, or utilitarian, ethics which is based on consequences; and *aretaic*, or virtue, ethics which is based on character formation (Pojman 2000). Pojman's definitions are as follows: "*Utilitarianism* [teleological, or utilitarian, ethics], which aims at maximizing good consequences, usually defined in terms of pleasure or happiness; *deontological ethics*, which focuses on the individual act (its inherent rightness or wrongness) and the individual (his or her inherent dignity or value); and *virtue ethics*, which focuses on character, the kind of qualities we should inculcate, the kind of people we should become" (3).

Aristotle believed in the study of ethics and the study of politics, which he considered as inseparable. He espoused the concept of happiness, *eudaimona*, by which people live a flourishing life, one that is filled with meaning and contentment. To Aristotle, technical excellence and moral excellence are complementary, and to this end he encouraged people to live by ethical principles and virtues, and practice as one integrated whole (Frankena 1956; cf. also Sison 2006, 108–21).

"Virtue ethics declares its task as focusing on what is important to the individual and society in contemporary life, which occurs in patterns of interaction" (McEwan 2001, 91). "[V]irtue is a habit, but not a mindless one. You act virtuously with the intent to do the right thing" (Ciulla 2003, 55).

The assumption that virtue ethics makes is: "good people (those of high moral character) make good moral choices" (Johnson 2005, 66). Virtue ethicists start with a portrait of the ideal person in mind, in this instance, a leader; identify the worthwhile qualities or tendencies that make up the character of this ethical ideal; and suggest means to achieve it. According to Johnson (2005), there are three main characteristics of virtues: virtues are interwoven into the lives of the inner core of leaders and persist over long stretches of time; virtues shape both the way leaders view things and the way they behave, and hence they weigh issues in ethical fashion and act morally; and virtues operate independently of circumstances (as opposed to situational ethics), i.e., their actions are principled, not swayed by popularity or timidity. The primary virtues as advocated by Aristotle and Plato are prudence (discernment, discretion), justice (righteousness, integrity), courage (strength in the face of adversity), and self-restraint (temperance) (67–68). James Rest (1986) identifies four thought processes that help moral leaders act upon their convictions: moral sensitivity, moral assessment, moral motivation (will or courage), and moral action that is congruent with moral values. Moral sensitivity involves the recognition that a situation raises ethical concerns; moral assessment involves the determining of an ethical course of action; moral motivation identifies the values that should determine priorities to consider in the decision; and moral action is acting on ethical decisions made regardless of consequences.

Deontological Ethics

Frankena (2002), in his critique of virtue ethics, argues that virtue alone is insufficient to enact a moral act. It requires principles to bring the virtue out into practice. Morality is a combination of being (virtue ethics) and doing (deontological ethics), or what he calls "morality of traits" and "morality of principles" (Frankena 1973, cited in Pojman 2002b, 352–53). These two ethical theories—virtue and deontology—are complementary aspects of the same morality: "For every principle there will be a morally good trait, often going by the same name, consisting of a disposition or tendency to act according to it; and for every morally good trait there will be a principle defining the kind of action in which it is to express itself. [P]rinciples without traits are impotent and traits without principles are blind" (Frankena, 352).

Deontological ethics is a system based on principles in which actions, or character, or even intentions are considered inherently right or wrong. This rightness or wrongness of the action is determined intrinsically, and *not* by its consequences (Pojman 2000, 293–94). Immanuel Kant (1724–1804), the great German philosopher, presents deontological ethics as "categorical imperative"—that is, an act can be tested for its moral status if it can be stated as a principle for universal application. "Ethics is not *contingent* but *absolute*, and its duties or imperatives are not *hypothetical* but *categorical* (non-conditional)" (Kant, translated by T. K. Abbott 1873; and cited in Pojman 2000, 298). Kant's deontological ethic is based on three premises: (1) an action must be done from a sense of duty in order to have moral worth; (2) the action done out of duty is based on volition, not coercion; and (3) the action is based on a universal moral obligation (categorical imperative) that every rational being is in agreement with. Deontological ethics, according to Kant, is not based on religion, but on reason alone.

Utilitarian Ethics (or Teleological Ethics)

This third kind of ethical system comes from the Greek word *teleos* meaning "having reached one's end . . . in which the locus of value is the outcome or consequences of the act" (Pojman 2002b, 107). One type of teleological ethics is known as ethical egoism, the view that it is the right act when the agent of the act receives the most benefit from it. Another type of teleological ethics prescribes that the right act is when the society derives greatest good from that act (i.e., the greatest amount of good for the greatest amount of people). This type of teleological ethics is also known as utilitarian ethics.

As a moral philosophy, utilitarianism was first introduced through the works of Scottish philosophers Frances Hutcheson (1694–1746), David Hume (1711–1776), and Adam Smith (1723–1790) and became classical philosophical theories through the English social reformers Jeremy Bentham (1748–1832) and John Stuart Mill (1806–1873). Bentham's concern for the English masses was more practical than theoretical: "An act is right if it either brings about more pleasure than pain or prevents pain, and an act is wrong if it either brings about more pain than pleasure or prevents pleasure from occurring" (Pojman 2002b, 109).

There are two types of utilitarianism—act-utilitarianism and rule-utilitarianism. The former refers to an act that is considered right when its results effect as much good as any other alternative; while the latter is considered right when its results "lead to greater utility for society than any available alternative" (Pojman 2002b, 112).

Seen from these definitions, utilitarian ethics does have positive outcomes: (1) it is a single principle that seems to be applicable to every situation; and (2) it appeals to our moral makeup that is not so much about rules but about helping people attain happiness and alleviate sufferings. However, utilitarian ethics also suffer from some deficiencies: (1) it is difficult to evaluate consequences, if not impossible all together (expectations are different and outcomes will vary from one situation to another); (2) it is difficult to be objective; "we tend to favor ourselves. . . . It is all too easy to confuse the 'greatest good' with our selfish interest" (Johnson 2005, 131); and (3) ironically, the greatest strength of utilitarian ethics is also the greatest weakness—when we think of what is best for the group as a whole, "utilitarianism discounts the worth of the individual" (Johnson 2007, 7).

Thomas Maak and Nicola M. Pless (2006) argue for responsible leadership (i.e., ethical or moral leadership which is not just being an effective, visionary, and good manager, but also having sound values and principles, and a good character) (34). There are four core dimensions of such responsible leadership: (1) the leader as a responsible person; (2) the role a responsible leader fulfills; (3) the ethics of the leader-follower relationship; and (4) the ethics of what a leader does (33–53). Citing the philosophical underpinnings of Aristotle, they assert that:

> [D]oing the right thing is not sufficient, that our character and virtues have to match and that we have to *live* what is good and desirable. . . . What we find, then, is that a leader does not have to be a moral hero but has to be a moral person (like everyone else). She should have certain moral qualities that make her a good person and show her integrity. Trust by followers is what follows. We note, thus, that a responsible leader should have *character* (having the right values and showing a firm—but not unchangeable—moral personality); be led by desirable *virtues* and principles such as respect, care, service, honesty, accountability, humility, trust, citizenship, respectful communication; and should practise *introspection* (citing George 2003). There are some hidden moral qualities or core dimensions of *ethical intelligence* that enable character building and living morality: *moral awareness*, *reflection skills* and *critical thinking* and *moral imagination*. (Maak and Pless 2006, 43, italics authors')

CCL AS RULE-UTILITARIAN IN ITS ETHICAL ORIENTATION

There are four reasons why CCL is tied to rule-utilitarian ethics. *First*, the national cultural dimensions (the Confucian values and worldview behind the practices of paternalistic authority (cf. pp. 23–39)) suggest that CCL operates on the basis of rule-utilitarian ethics.

According to Hofstede's study on national cultures (1980), Confucian societies share two national cultural dimensions known as high (or large) power distance and collectivism. These two dimensions parallel the twin outcomes of paternalistic authority: compliance (high power distance) and harmony (collectivism).

Power distance (PD) may be defined as "the extent to which the less powerful members of institutions and organizations within a country expect and accept that power is distributed unequally" (28). High (or large) PD describes the culture's willingness to accept social inequality, particularly related to authority and power. Low or small PD describes the culture's preference for consultation and interdependence between superior and subordinate.

The dimension of individualism vs. collectivism describes the relationship between the individual and others in the society. In countries with high individualism index scores, relationships with one another are loosely structured. In countries with high collectivism, relationships are tightly structured. People in such countries are integrated from birth into strong, cohesive, in-groups (vs. out-groups), which protect them throughout their lifetime in exchange for unquestioning loyalty (51).

In such societies, power and status are ascribed (cf. Browaeys and Price 2008). The effects of Hofstede's two of five national cultural dimensions in Confucian Asia, namely high power distance and collectivist, in relation to management and leadership are such that the organizational structure is a hierarchical pyramid, participative management is not possible, and ethics/values are particularistic rather than universalistic (Browaeys and Price 2008, 26). Particularism is a doctrine in which circumstances and relationships as being more important than absolutes; while universalism is a doctrine in which absolutes apply, irrespective of circumstances and situations (Browaeys and Price 2008, 83; cf. discussion on ethical orientation of Confucian Asian business leaders which are "relationship-based" and "role-based" as opposed to "dignity-based" in Koehn and Leung 2004, 265–372).

According to the Global Leadership and Organizational Behavior (GLOBE) study of sixty-two cultures, there are ten clusters of regional countries based on societal cultures (House et al. 2004, 190). Singapore, Hong Kong, Taiwan, China, South Korea, and Japan are classified as "Confucian Asia" because "[t]he teachings and works of Confucius, and later Buddha, had a distinct historical influence on the Confucian cluster" (188). Based on the nine cultural dimensions of the GLOBE study (194) "Confucian Asia societal cluster is characterized by practices of higher Performance Orientation, Institutional Collectivism, and In-Group Collectivism. The goals are collective and family-oriented, and rewards are significant for performance toward meeting collective goals" (200).

Second, from our previous discussion on the three key elements of CCL, it is evident that the different facets and key practices and strategies of contemporary PA tend the leader more toward an authoritarian than benevolent or moral posture (cf. pp. 36–39). This is heavily substantiated by literature available on this subject. The authoritarian nature and posture of CCL conforms most to "rule utilitarian" ethics rather than virtue or deontological ethics. "[A]uthoritarianism in Chinese culture is rooted in the paramount value of submission to authority" (Farh and Cheng 2000, 113). However, Farh and Cheng observe that this "pillar of traditional Chinese culture" has been challenged by Western-led modernization in China and Taiwan.

Third, the practice of paternalistic authority in CCL may not be classified as deontological ethics. Given the predominance of authoritarianism over benevolence and moral character, most of the facets and practices of PA cannot be classified as principles for universal application according to Kantian "categorical imperative[s]." Many of the "ethical" values of CCL, in general, are particularistic rather than universal—they are heavily dependent on contexts, persons, and situations (cf. Hooker 2003). As Westwood points out, the Confucian leader needs to be seen as moral, "[n]ot 'moral' in the sense of conformance to high or universal principles, but rather of behaving within situations and relationships in culturally required and expected ways" (Westwood 1997, 467). It is clear from the extant literature that benevolence or "paternalistic individualized care" as a virtue in its various forms and practices does exist in the Confucian leader and follower relationship. However, the practice of benevolence as a leadership virtue in Confucian society needs to be understood in context—benevolence is given in return for compliance and harmony. In this regard, benevolence inclines toward rule-utilitarian ethics, rather than virtue or deontological ethics.

Farh and Cheng (2000) make the point that expected reciprocity of obligation and mutuality in the relationship between the superior and the subordinate may not be symmetrical: "The tradition of Three Bonds [father and son; husband and wife; elder brother and younger brother] has made it clear that even when superiors behave in contradiction to their role requirements, inferiors are still expected to fulfill their role obligations. . . . Moreover, given the authoritarian role of the father, a father's benevolence does not necessarily translate into his responsiveness to the psychological needs of the son" (104–105).

Fourth, it is our claim that the moral dimension of paternalistic authority is weak. It can be argued that this moral dimension is not uniformly or consistently applied in terms of degrees among the three key elements of PA, namely, authoritarianism, benevolence, and moral character. Hence, virtue ethics seems to be the weakest dimension in CCL. As far as the extant literature goes, many authors and writers have difficulty in articulating clearly and succinctly how the contemporary Confucian leader exercises moral leadership. Some of them assume that it is a given "inborn" trait characteristic of the human fabric in Confucian society, and hence in their research they claim that moral character is seldom mentioned by their respondents because it is an assumed value in their culture. The fact that it is least mentioned does not mean that it is inherently present in those who are interviewed. I contend that argument from silence is less than credible. However, I understand that moral character has always been championed as the Confucian ideal, but in reality and practice, I believe that this is the weakest stance of the three elements in the exercise of PA (i.e., authoritarianism is the overriding stance in contemporary Confucian leadership). On the other hand, credit must be given to most of these authors and writers who espouse morality or ethics as a basic requirement for Confucian leadership, but they are hard put in their research to specifically define what moral or ethical leadership looks like for the contemporary Confucian leader today. They understand the Confucian ideal; they assume that moral character is highest among the three elements of PA, but they have not shown sufficient proof to demonstrate that it is the overriding stance over authoritarianism (cf. 23–36). Farh and Cheng (2000), acknowledge that there are still unresolved issues concerning moral leadership in Confucian Asia—their research is limited to PRC and Taiwan, and only two virtues are mentioned: "avoid acting selfishly" and "lead by example" (116). What about other Confucian societies in East and Southeast Asia?—are there more important virtues concerning moral leadership? How do subordinates form impressions about leader's moral integrity? What impact would leader morality have on followers?

While I am *not* saying that there is no hint of virtue ethics or deontological ethics at play in the practice of PA in CCL; these ethical theories are not as prominent as rule-utilitarian ethics in the practices of PA in CCL. Given the Confucian values, worldviews, and practices of PA in CCL, I can *assuredly* classify CCL under "rule-utilitarian" ethics.

Differences between ICL and CCL

The above section demonstrates that CCL, with its tendencies toward authoritarianism over benevolence and moral character, inclines toward a rule-utilitarian ethical orientation which exposes its weakness—the susceptibility to abuse power and authority in leadership. Comparing CCL and ICL, the differences between these two patterns of Confucian leadership become very apparent, both in ethical orientation as well as in practice (cf. table 3.2, p. 48). ICL is oriented toward virtue ethics (cf. discussion in chapter 2), while CCL is oriented toward rule-utilitarian ethics.

Cheung and Chan (2005), in their study of Chinese philosophical foundations (Confucianistic, Daoist, Mohist, and Legalist doctrines) among five prominent businessmen in Hong Kong, comment about Idealized Confucian leadership: "[T]he success of Confucian ethics requires that every person is a gentleman [superior man]; . . . [t]his assumption proves so idealistic that Confucians recognize the limit of their ethics, that they are not applicable to uncultivated people. . . . [T]he virtuous Confucian doctrines can be impractical and rhetorical" (59). They argue for the use of other Chinese philosophical doctrines such as the "Daoist ethics of nonintervention," "Mohist ethics of altruism," and "Legalist ethics of impartiality;" since "[idealized or classical] Confucian ethics are prone to be moralistic, impractical, and conservative" (58).

CORRELATING CCL WITH YUKL'S CRITERIA FOR ETHICAL LEADERSHIP

Yukl (2002) made the observation that judgments in leadership about the ethics of a particular action or decision has to bring three factors into consideration: purpose (ends), the level of behavior that is consistent with moral standards (means), and how that decision affects self and others (consequences). These three factors are critical in discerning a decision or action as either ethical or unethical, and "the common issue is the extent to which the end justifies the means" (402). Yukl provides a helpful list of eight criteria to evaluate ethical leadership: use of leader power and influence, handling the diverse interests of the multiple stakeholders, development of a vision for the organization, integrity of leader behavior, risk taking in leader decisions and actions, communication of relevant information about operations, response to criticism and dissent by followers, and development of follower skills and self confidence (406).

TABLE 3.2. Comparison and Contrast between ICL and CCL

	ICL	CCL		
Posture of power and authority	Superior man (cf. ch. 2)	Authoritarian-Paternalistic (cf. table 3.1 p. 30)		
		Authoritarianism	Benevolent	Moral
Practices of power and authority	Rule of Virtue: (*Te*) benefit the people (appeal to their self respect and not fear) (De Bary 1989, 6) Rule of Love: (*Ren*) has the interests of the people at heart, and not self interest and personal gain	Authority and control: Underestimation of subordinate competence Reputation building of self Didactic leadership Centralization of control Ambivalent stance: non-emotional ties and social distance Protection of dominance: high control, low trust Abuse and misuse of power and authority Corruption Patronage and nepotism Cronyism	Idealized care: Treat employees as family; provide job security, assistance during personal crises, holistic concern, protection to employees from embarrassment in public Overlook even grave mistakes of subordinates	Unselfishness: Authority not abused for selfish gain Keep private business interest separate Put collective interest ahead of personal interest Lead by example
Ethical system	Moral-virtuous	Rule-utilitarian		

In applying Yukl's evaluative criteria to CCL, and in relation to Westwood and Chua's Nine Strategies of Paternalistic Authority, the correlation is charted in table 3.3. More than half of the facets and practices associated with CCL fall under what Yukl terms as "unethical leadership." These are in the areas of centralization of authority, patronage and nepotism, cliques and political manipulation, corruption, reputation building and networking, personalism, protection of dominance, non-emotional ties and social distance, aloofness and social distance, conveying non-specific intentions to avoid explicit stance, didactic leadership, dependence orientation of subordinates.

TABLE 3.3. Correlation between Yukl's Eight Criteria for Evaluating Ethical Leadership and CCL's Paternalistic Authoritarian Facets and Practices (adapted from Yukl 2002, 406).

Yukl's eight criteria for ethical leadership	Yukl's elaboration of unethical leadership	Labels for CCL (Westwood et al. 1992, 1997; Farh and Cheng 2000; Lowe 2003; Silin 1976; Redding 1993)
Use of leader power and influence	Satisfies personal needs and career objectives	Reputation building and networking
Handling the diverse interests of the multiple stake holders	Favors coalition partners who offer the most personal gain	Patronage and nepotism Cliques, political manipulation Cronyism and corruption
Development of a vision for the organization	Attempts to sell a personal vision as the only way for the organization to succeed	Lack of organizational vision
Integrity of leader behavior	Does what is expedient for attaining personal objectives	Personalism Non-emotional ties and social distance
Risk taking in leader decisions and actions	Avoids necessary decisions or actions that involve personal risk to the leader	Aloofness and social distance Conveying non-specific intentions to avoid explicit stance
Communication of relevant information about operations	Uses deception and distortion to bias follower perceptions about problems and progress	Didactic leadership
Response to criticism and dissent by followers	Discourages and suppresses any criticism or dissent	Centralization of authority Protection of dominance through various subtle tactics
Development of follower skills and self-confidence	De-emphasizes development to keep followers weak and dependent on the leader	Dependence orientation of subordinates

SUMMARY

The nature of Contemporary (Practiced) Confucian Leadership or Contemporary Confucian Leadership (CCL), which is predominantly paternalistic-authoritarian with a shade of benevolence and moral obligation, falls short as ethical leadership due to its inclination toward rule-utilitarian ethics.

First, I discussed the nature of Contemporary (Practiced) Confucian Leadership (CCL) in terms of three leadership elements: authoritarianism, benevolence, and moral character. These are key elements under the broad contemporary Confucian leadership style known as paternalistic authority (PA). The literature base demonstrates that the contemporary exercise of PA is prevalent in societies that have been heavily influenced by Confucian values. The three elements of CCL are discussed alongside its cultural roots.

Second, I highlighted several facets of PA, and the leadership practices or strategies in CCL they entail. These facets and strategies are characteristic of the authoritarian, benevolent, and moral posture of the contemporary Confucian leader, with authoritarian leadership as the predominant feature. These practices expose CCL's weakest link: the moral element of PA.

Third, I examined CCL from the perspective of the three predominant moral and ethical theories—virtue ethics, deontological ethics, and utilitarian ethics (a subset of teleological ethics)—to determine the ethical theory that is most closely aligned with CCL. The analysis is that CCL operates along the lines of rule-utilitarian ethics. While utilitarian ethics does have its strengths, there are limitations which render the predominant authoritarian stance in CCL as inadequate for ethical leadership.

Fourth, I captured the major differences between the two patterns of Confucian leadership, namely, ICL and CCL. ICL's ethical orientation is aligned with virtue ethics, while CCL's ethical orientation is geared toward rule-utilitarian ethics.

Fifth, I correlated the nine practices and strategies of CCL with Gary Yukl's eight ethical criteria for evaluating ethical leadership (2002). This correlation reveals that more than half of CCL's facets and practices of PA fall under Yukl's criteria of "unethical leadership."

In chapter 4 my proposition is that, based on social science leadership theories and power-influence theories, CCL is insufficient as a theory in practice because CCL tends to exercise coercive and reward power bases which point toward self-interest above others. In chapter 5 I argue that CCL falls short of ethical values and practices that are based on the teachings of Jesus Christ.

4

Ethical/Moral Leadership as Normative Practice: CCL and its Deficiencies

> Leadership is morality magnified. Unlike individual morality, the morality of a leader ripples through organizations, communities and societies. We know that leaders have the potential to inflict great harm or bestow great benefits on their constituents. When leader errs, many people suffer. Leadership is a specific type of human relationship and ethics is about the way we treat each other in various relationships. (Ciulla 2006, 17)

MORAL OR ETHICAL LEADERSHIP is normative for the understanding and practice of leadership in any field of life. This chapter serves to describe and demonstrate the significance of moral leadership as normative practice from social science research.

Rhode (2006), the editor of *Moral Leadership: The Theory and Practice of Power, Judgment, and Policy*, argues for the efficacy of ethical leadership in today's business. Along with other contributors in her edited work, Rhodes offers a workable definition of moral leadership as that of "exercising influence in ways that are ethical in means and ends. . . . [E]ffective leadership requires a moral dimension too often missing or marginal in American business and professional organizations" (9).

POWER-INFLUENCE THEORIES

Power-influence theorists view power as the primary characteristic dominant in the relationship between the leader and follower. This approach to understanding leadership began in the 1950s and continues to dominate leadership literature today. There are two approaches in power-influence theory: the social power approach and the social exchange approach. There are three essential questions: How does the leader view the concept of power or authority? How does the leader acquire power or authority? How does the leader use power or authority in leadership practice—what is its impact on followership, and responses to such practices?

Social Power Approach to Leadership: Five Power Bases

French and Raven (1959) were among the first to discover and identify the different bases of power that could be used to influence or lead others. Their theory on power refers to the ability of an agent to influence a target. Power may be understood as influence on another person toward change in behavior, opinion, and attitude. They proposed five bases of power that are used to lead others: legitimate power, reward power, coercive power, expert power, and referent power. The first three power bases may be classified as position power, which is determined largely by an organization's policies and procedures, while the last two power bases are known as personal power (Lim and Daft 2004, 468).

Legitimate power may be defined as the right to influence or prescribe another person's behavior. This may be perceived as authority granted through a formal position in an organization. For example, when someone becomes a supervisor, subordinates understand that they are to take instructions from their supervisor; they are obligated to follow his or her instructions with respect to work activities. The subordinates accept this power base as legitimate, which is why they comply.

Reward power refers to the capacity to provide others with things they desire or value; for example, appointed leaders may be in a position to give away formal rewards such as pay increases or promotions. Leaders who operate from this power base have great leverage to influence subordinates' behavior.

Coercive power refers to the leader's authority to remove rewards or privileges or to administer sanctions and punishment. Supervisors can use coercive power to criticize, reprimand, or demote subordinates. Coercive power can be seen as the negative side of legitimate and reward power.

Expert power refers to the leader's special knowledge or skill that he or she has over the followers in performing a task. The leader can provide subordinates with needed information, knowledge, or expertise that they may not have. The leader can withhold information to influence or achieve particular desired outcomes.

Referent power refers to the leader's ability to provide others with feelings of personal acceptance, approval, efficacy, or worth. In other words, the leader with referent power commands the followers' respect, identification, and willing followership so that they want to emulate the leader. Referent power does not depend on a formal title or position, but on the leader's personal characteristics.

Based on the research of McClelland and Burnham (1995) and the social power typology of French and Raven (1959), Kanungo and Mendoca (1996) illustrate the relationship between the moral value of altruism and use of power. At the same time, they demonstrate the difference between an ethically principled leader and one who is not:

> In a sense, the need for power explains why influence or control is exercised, and the power base explains how it is exercised. The impact of these concepts on understanding leader behavior is quite significant. To exercise influence over their followers, leaders who are high in personal power need are likely to use more often their position power base—that is, the use of resources such as rights of one's office, ability to exercise coercion, and control over rewards. On the other hand, leaders who are high in the institutional power need are likely to influence their followers more often by the use of their personal power base—that is, the expertise or attraction as perceived by the followers. (47)

In relating the concept of power motivation to moral altruism, the authors claim that "individuals high on personal power need are preoccupied with their own interests and concerns" (47). Such behaviors are pursued at the cost of the organization's welfare and effectiveness, and such power wielding leaders demand and expect followers' loyalty to feed their own personal agendas and goals. These are the kinds of leaders who will use positional power bases such as coercion, legal means, and reward, to get their own way. Their underlying motive is that of egotism to satisfy their self-aggrandizement, and they use high control to get their way. Various authors have written on this subject of dysfunctional leadership (e.g., Kets de Vries and Miller 1997, 195–214; Conger 1997, 215–32, Vecchio 1997; Kellerman 2004; Kelman and Hamilton 1989; Lipman-Blumen 2005).

Conversely, the kind of leaders who have high institutional power need has the interests of the organization and its members at heart. They place their personal self-interest under that of the organization "which then becomes the sole reason for their desire to influence and control others" (48). These leaders help shape and streamline the organization toward fulfilling the organization's mission and vision. Such leaders draw upon their personal power base—that is, expertise or attraction as perceived by the followers. They use reward power or sanctions sparingly. For them, "power becomes the vehicle to serve the needs of the organization and its members." Their modus operandi is empowerment instead of control of members. They use referent and expert power bases to bring about organizational effectiveness in fulfilling their mission and objectives.

Contemporary Confucian leaders, however, engage largely in legitimate, reward, and coercive power bases, and their leadership is characterized by the ills of these power bases. Using French and Raven's typology of power bases, table 4.1, p. 56 shows the types of power bases from which CCL operates. The authoritarian component of CCL engages legitimate and coercive power bases in its multiple strategies and practices. The benevolent component engages reward power base, referring to the rewards conferred on those who are favored by the contemporary Confucian leader. However, CCL is not totally problematic. Engaging referent power base in the moral-obligatory component, the CCL leader brings harmony to people—building goodwill between the leader and the follower, and among followers.

There are three outcomes as a result of the use of the five power bases: compliance, resistance, and commitment. When leaders successfully use position power (legitimate, reward, and coercive), the natural response is compliance. Yukl (2002) describes compliance as "an outcome in which the target [follower] is willing to do what the agent [leader] asks but is apathetic rather than enthusiastic about it and will make only minimal effort" (143). Lim and Daft (2004) add that "if the use of position power, especially the use of coercion, exceeds a level people consider legitimate, people may resist the attempt to influence" (471).

Resistance refers to subordinates not wanting to carry out the orders of their leader. Six possible scenarios of resistance are painted by Yukl (2002) when subordinates resist the overtures of their leader: they make excuses; they negotiate with the agent; they seek higher authority to overrule the request; they intentionally delay the request; they may sabotage the task assigned to them; or they downright refuse to carry out the request.

Commitment is the usual response that followers adopt when their leader exercises personal power (expert and referent). Commitment refers to followers' willingness to carry out the request and implement it enthusiastically and effectively.

TABLE 4.1. CCL in Relation to French and Raven's Power Bases

French and Raven's power bases	CCL: Practices and strategies of paternalistic authority (cf. discussion in chapter 3) [Asterisk * indicates positive aspect of CCL]
Legitimate power	Centralization of control, personalism Dependence orientation of subordinates
Reward power	Benevolence Patronage and nepotism Reputation building and networking Non-emotional ties and social distance
Coercive power	Authoritarianism Cliques and political manipulation through divide-and-rule Corruption Protection of dominance through various subtle tactics Aloofness and social distance Conveying non-specific intentions to avoid explicit stance Didactic leadership
Expert power	--
Referent power	*Moral-obligatory *Harmony building Conflict resolution through face-saving tactics Dialogue ideal

Kellerman (2008), in his book *Followership: How Followers are Creating Change and Changing Leaders*, gives a good literature review about the subject on followership. She surveyed the works of Abraham Zaleznik (1965), Abraham Zaleznik and Manfred F. R. Kets de Vries (1975); Robert Kelley (1992); Ira Chaleff (2003); and her own descriptive analyses between followers and leaders from the arena of political science. Kellerman's typology of followership distinguishes good followers and bad followers based on two overriding criteria—means and ends. The former relates to the level of engagement (some engagement being better than none), while the latter relates to motivation (public interest is better than self-interest). Kellerman formulates five axioms that are worth considering concerning morality and ethics in terms of followership: (1) To do nothing—to be not involved at all—is to be a bad follower; (2) To support a leader who is good—effective and ethical—is to be a good follower; (3) To support a leader who is bad—ineffective and/or unethical—is to be a bad follower; (4) To oppose a leader who is good—effective and ethical—is to be a bad follower; and (5) To oppose a leader who is bad—ineffective and or/unethical—is to be a good follower (229–30).

Kellerman's definitions of a follower is a "subordinate who has less power, authority, and influence than do their superiors;" and followership is "the relationship between a subordinate and a superior, *as well as* the response of the former to the latter" (235). She emphasizes the values about followership rather than about followers, and hence her thesis is that "*followers are more important to leaders than leaders are to followers*" (242, italics author's). She makes six important assumptions that I believe are moral statements that have great impact for the way we understand ethical leadership, or more accurately, moral followership: (1) Followers form a group with members who share a common interest; (2) While followers, by definition, lack authority; however, they do not by definition lack power and influence; (3) Followers are agents of change; (4) Followers "ought to support good leadership and thwart bad leadership"; (5) Followers who do something about their situation are more preferred to those who do nothing about it; and (6) Followers can bring about change by "circumventing their leaders and joining other followers instead" (239–43).

Robert E. Kelley (1992) describes five styles of followership through extensive interviews with leaders and followers. These styles of followership are categorized according to two dimensions as illustrated in figure 4.1, p. 58. The first dimension deals with followers who are considered independent and critical thinking versus dependent and uncritical thinking. Lim and Daft (2004) give succinct descriptions of these two groups of followers: "[The former] are aware of the significance of their own actions and actions of others. They can weigh the impact of decisions on the vision set forth by a leader and offer constructive criticism, creativity, and innovation. Conversely, a dependent, uncritical thinker does not consider possibilities beyond what he or she is told, does not contribute to the cultivation of the organization, and accepts the leader's ideas without question" (248).

The second dimension of follower style, according to Kelley, is that the former followers (independent and critical thinking) are active versus the latter (dependent and uncritical thinking) who are passive. From these two dimensions, five styles of followership are proposed: an alienated follower, a passive follower, a conformist, a pragmatic survivor, or an effective follower.

Figure 4.1. Kelley's styles of followership (adapted from Kelley 1992, 97).

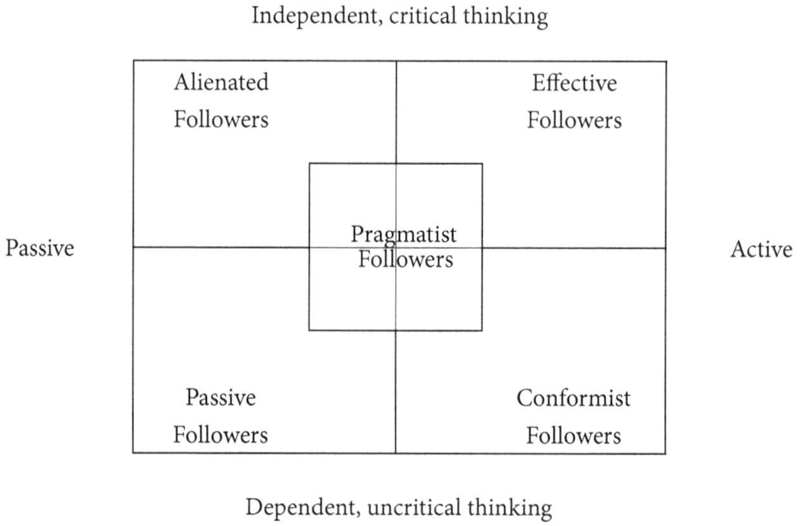

Independent, critical thinking

Alienated Followers

Effective Followers

Passive

Pragmatist Followers

Active

Passive Followers

Conformist Followers

Dependent, uncritical thinking

The alienated follower is a passive, yet independent, critical thinker. They are often effective followers who have experienced setbacks and obstacles, perhaps promises broken by superiors. They are capable, but they choose to dwell on the shortcomings of the organization and people—they do not participate in developing solutions to the problems they see.

The conformist (follower) is a "yes" man or "yes" woman who follows orders regardless of the nature of the task given. The conformist does not consider the consequences of their compliant behavior even at the risk of being a contributor to unhealthy endeavor or activity. They avoid conflicts at all cost, and seldom contribute to the progress and advancement of the organization. The pragmatic follower or survivor has qualities of all four extremes—the chameleon who adapts to whatever situation that works to his or her advantage, and minimizes risk. Pragmatists are found in organizations that are struggling to survive and there are about 25 to 35 per cent of followers who tend toward this style, "avoiding risks and fostering the status qua, often for political reasons" (Lim and Daft, 250).

The passive follower demonstrates neither critical, independent thinking nor active participation. They show no initiative or a sense of responsibility. They require a great deal of supervision and usually are compliant without any resistance to authority.

The effective follower is both a critical, independent thinker, as well as an active participant in the organization. Effective followers are not afraid of risk taking, nor are they afraid to deal with conflicts when they arise. They are courageous to initiate change and put themselves at risk with others' views, even their leaders, to serve the best interest of the organization. Lim and Daft describe effective followers as people who are "[c]haracterized by both mindfulness and a willingness to act; effective followers are essential for an organization to be effective. They are capable of self-management, they discern strengths and weaknesses in themselves and in the organization, they are committed to something larger than themselves, and they work toward competency, solutions, and positive impact. Effective followers are far from powerless—and they know it. Therefore, they do not despair in their positions, nor do they resent or manipulate others" (250).

Kelley's (1992) typology of followership differentiates the kinds of followers according to the kinds of leaders who lead them. Teachings by Jesus in the New Testament that is ethical leadership (cf. later discussion on social exchange theory below) encourages effective followership. Followers become "effective followers" because their human worth is respected and they are given space to develop critical and independent thinking, hence, they act in accordance to ethical leadership. On the contrary, CCL with its propensity toward authoritarian, benevolent, and obligatory moral stance encourages uncritical thinking, passive, and conformist followers. CCL evokes pragmatic followers who follow any kind of leadership that work to their advantage.

In all likelihood, CCL "discourages" the alienated followers who otherwise have a great deal to contribute but feel alienated because of the positional power bases (mainly coercive and legitimate power bases) that CCL adopts in its use toward followers (cf. figure 4.1, p. 58). Alienated followers are made to feel as if they are unworthy human beings who function like "cogs in a machine." Alienated followers eschew a culture of dependence, much against the cultural and management ethos of CCL.

In the light of our understanding about the various styles of followership, CCL, with its predominant stance of authoritarianism, benevolence, obligatory, and moral disposition, encourages uncritical thinking, passive, and conformist followership. The consequence of exercising CCL is compliance, not commitment. At its worst, it leads to resistance in one form or another as demonstrated in history.

Social Exchange Approach to Leadership: Transactional and Transformational Leadership

Transactional leadership can be understood as a relationship between the leader and follower which fulfills the needs of both. The means of exchange between the leader and follower are usually in the form of economic, political, or psychological rewards. One example is when a potential political leader promises jobs to followers in exchange for votes to enable the potential leader to be elected to political office.

Transactional behavior focuses on the accomplishment of tasks and good subordinate relationships in exchange for mutually beneficial and desirable rewards. This leader–member exchange relationship may in turn encourage the leader to adapt styles and behaviors to suit the perceived or real expectations of followers. This implies that followers, too, have the potential to influence the leader in a two-way exchange. Transactional leadership manifests four leadership behaviors that correspond closely to the power typology of French and Raven (1959): contingent reward, passive management by exception, active management by exception, and laissez-faire leadership.

Contingent reward implies that leaders use rewards or incentives as means to achieve their goals, and this corresponds with French and Raven's position power, namely, reward power. The use of contingent reward or reward power leads to compliance as power rests with the leader to provide desirable rewards for expectations met.

Passive management by exception implies that leaders use correction or punishment in response to unacceptable behavior or performance or a deviation from standard practice. This management style corresponds to French and Raven's position power, namely, coercive power. This type of power when used to influence followers stems from the followers' fear of punishment or negative consequences that may befall them if they fail to comply.

Active management by exception implies that leaders actively monitor the work performances of followers and use corrective actions to ensure that work is completed according to standard procedures and expected outcomes. This type of management corresponds to French and Raven's legitimate and coercive power bases.

Laissez-faire management demonstrates a leader's abdication of responsibility to lead. This "hands off" approach to leadership speaks of an ineffective style of leadership and it can be seen in various ways. The leader does not respond to the needs of the followers; the leader does not take appropriate steps to respond to problems arising out of his sphere of leadership; the leader does not bother to monitor the performance of followers on task.

Transformational leadership, however, has higher and nobler goals and is regarded as more influential in the leadership process. Transformational leadership may be seen as a higher ideal in that it surpasses that of meeting the basic needs of the followers. It is seen as a partnership between the leader and the led in which the follower is raised or transformed to a higher level of motivation and morality (Burns 1978).

Much has been written on transactional versus transformational leadership (e.g., Bass 1990; Bennis and Nanus 1985). The major difference between these two forms of leadership lies in the skills of the leader to fulfill or even exceed the expectations and desires of the followers. Bass (1985) asserts that transactional leadership works best within a maintenance mode whereby the organization culture is maintained without much change. Transformational leadership sees the need to change the culture through invention, introduction and advancement of new cultural values and forms that will transform the followers as well as the environment in which they work.

Bass (1985) acknowledges that the genesis of the social exchange theory on leadership rightly belongs to Burns (1978). However, he builds on Burns' idea and brings it to another level of understanding transformational leadership. According to Bass, transformational leaders transform and motivate the followers to feel trust, admiration, loyalty, and respect toward the leader. The followers are motivated to go beyond their basal needs and are highly motivated to do more than the bare minimum. The motivation for followers to achieve higher levels of performance lies in the significance of the task at hand. The emphasis is on team building and team achievement rather than on self-interest and personal gains. What Burns promulgated as a morally uplifting form of leadership has been further developed by Bass' emphasis on innovational or motivational leadership.

The three primary characteristics associated with transformational leadership are charisma (Weber, 1947, first developed this concept), individual consideration, and intellectual stimulation. Bass and Avolio, in their later research (Yukl 2002), added inspiration (or the ability to articulate and cast a vision) and modeling appropriate behavior as the other essential characteristics of transformational leaders.

According to Bass, there are three essential traits to charismatic leaders: self-confidence, self-esteem, and self-determination. However, it does not mean that charismatic leaders are necessarily transformational leaders. Most leadership theorists share the view that charisma is more of an attributive factor that followers place on their leader. A leader is perceived as charismatic as a result of followers' perceptions and attribution, which are influenced by the leader's qualities (e.g., dominant, influential, possesses moral values) and behavior, the context, and the needs of the followers (Yukl 2002; Northouse 2004; Conger 1999; Conger and Kanungo 1998).

Some theorists use the terms charismatic leadership and transformational leadership interchangeably; while others claim that they are different, and that charismatic leaders are found in the contexts of crises (Weber 1947).

Bass and Steidmeier (2004) posit that the ethics of leadership rests upon three key pillars, namely, (1) the moral character of the leader; (2) the ethical legitimacy of the leader's values in the vision, communication, and direction; and (3) the moral process of social interactions between leader and follower (175). The authors' assumption is that "when [transformational] leaders are morally mature, those they lead display higher moral reasoning" (175–76). In their argument they compare and contrast moral issues between transactional leadership (TSL) and transformational leadership (TFL). While they acknowledge that most leaders display "mixed moral profile," their analyses of "authentic leaders" refer more to those who display higher levels of morality than others. For Burns (1978), to be a transformational leader is to be "morally uplifting," and for Bass (1985), it is "virtuous or villainous, depending on their values."

In their article, Bass and Steidmeier attempt to compare and contrast authentic and pseudo-transformational leadership in terms of the four components of TFL, namely, idealized influence or charisma, inspirational motivation, intellectual stimulation, and individualized consideration. This last component, individualized consideration, is the ultimate deciding component between a truly transformational leader and one who is not. Coaching, mentoring, and growth opportunities are given to the follower by the transformational leader (Bass 1985) to grow them into leaders.

According to Bass and Steidmeier, pseudo-transformational leaders "[are] concerned about maintaining dependence of their followers,"—"maintain deference from them;" "welcome and expect blind obedience;" "foment favoritism and competition among followers;" "maintain a parent-child relationship;" "use power primarily for self-aggrandizement;" "[are] predisposed toward self-serving biases;" "withhold the release of information;" and "engage in shams and pretenses" (182–83).

In contrast, authentic transformational leaders are those who are "true to self and others . . . characterized by high moral and ethical standards in each of the [four] dimensions" of transformational leadership (184). Such leaders "identify the core values and unifying purposes of the organization and its members, liberate their human potential, and foster pluralistic leadership and effective, satisfied followers" (193).

Kanungo and Mendoca (1996) depict transactional leadership in terms of five processes of influence and their respective moral or ethical implications (table 4.2, p. 64). Based on their analysis of the influence processes and ethical implications of transactional leadership, I attempt to correlate the practices and strategies of CCL with their framework. The result shows a correspondence between the five influence processes and the facets of CCL. This indicates that CCL is similar to transactional leadership, both in its nature as well as its ethical shortfalls. The use of coercive, legal, and reward power bases result in the characteristic high control of leaders, protection of dominance, manipulation, cronyism, corruption, and emphasis on compliant behavior, among other ills. Given these moral and ethical failures, CCL disqualifies itself as ethical leadership (cf. Hoyk and Hersey 2008).

TABLE 4.2. Correlation between CCL's Practices and Strategies of PA and Kanungo and Mendoca's Ethical Implications of Transactional Leadership Influence Processes (1996, 73).

Kanungo and Mendoca's leadership influence process	Kanungo and Mendoca's ethical implications of transactional leadership	Labels for CCL (cf. table 3.3, p. 49)
Strategies	Control	Centralization of control, personalism Non-emotional ties and social distance Reputation building and networking
Leadership objectives in terms of behavioral outcome	Emphasis on compliance behavior	Dependence orientation of subordinates
Underlying psychological mechanism	Social exchange of valued resources	Benevolence Patronage and nepotism
Power base	Coercive, legal, reward	Cliques and political manipulation Cronyism and corruption Protection of dominance through various subtle tactics Aloofness and social distance Conveying non-specific intentions to avoid explicit stance Didactic leadership
Attitude change process and effects	Compliance, which under excessive control, often leads to demolishing followers' self-worth and to their functioning as programmed robots	Uncritical, passive, dependent, conformist, alienated followers. (cf. figure 4.1, p. 58)

SUMMARY OF POWER-INFLUENCE THEORIES

The social power approach to leadership refers to how leaders influence their followers. The concept is heavily dependent on the seminal work of French and Raven (1959) who identified five power bases by which leaders influence their followers: legitimate, reward, coercive, expert, and referent. From their study, French and Raven suggest that the combined bases of expert power and referent power are believed to yield the greatest satisfaction and performance in followers and are used by leaders who are perceived as effective (Yukl 2002). Using the terminology of this social power approach, CCL's authoritarian-benevolent stance operates from a combination of legitimate, coercive, and reward power bases, marked by the use of positional power; while the obligatory-moral stance of CCL operates from a referent power base. The result is that CCL produces compliant followers, a moral failure that renders CCL ineffective as a leadership practice.

The social exchange approach to leadership can be described as a two-way exchange between the leader and the follower in which both are influenced to a large or small extent. The follower gives up his or her sense of autonomy or independence to allow for the leader to have authority over the follower and, in exchange, the leader provides the follower with rewards and benefits. Mapping CCL against Kanungo and Mendoca's (1996) framework on leadership influence processes, I conclude that CCL operates much the same way as transactional leadership in terms of influence mechanisms, and moral and ethical failures.

THE MORAL CHALLENGE OF POWER AND SELF-INTEREST

Conger (1997) discusses the temptations or pitfalls of highly effective leaders who manifest what he calls the "dark side of leadership." This happens when the leader loses sight of reality, becomes over exaggerated in his or her behavior, and seeking personal gains, unwittingly causes harm to the self and the followers, as well as the organization.

Manfred F. R. Kets de Vries and Danny Miller (1997) hypothesize about the relationship between the leader's narcissistic tendencies and their effectiveness—a dysfunction in leadership practice. "Narcissists feel they must rely on themselves rather than on others for the gratification of life's needs. . . . [They] become preoccupied with establishing their adequacy, power, beauty, status, prestige, and superiority" (199).

Barbara Kellerman (2004) seeks to answer the question as to why bad leadership exists. Kellerman claims that bad leadership falls into two categories: bad as in unethical and bad as in ineffective (32). She identifies seven types of such leadership that is prevalent today: incompetent, rigid, intemperate, callous, corrupt, insular, and evil. The first three types tend to be bad as in ineffective, and the last four tend to be bad as in unethical (39).

These two distinctive traits have to do with means (failure to distinguish between right and wrong—unethical) and end (failure to produce desired change—ineffective). Citing the call of James MacGregor Burn's (1978) to practice ethical and moral leadership, *transforming* leaders put the needs of the followers above their own; they exemplify virtues of courage and temperance, and they serve for the common good (34). The same is expected of followers: they hold their leaders to account, they exemplify virtues of courage and temperance, and they engage the leader and fellow followers in acting on behalf of the common good. Unethical followers, however, do not engage in any of the above ethical practices (36). Kellerman acknowledges that "[t]he mixture of the ineffective and the unethical in bad leadership can never be known or measured precisely. This is the truth of the human condition" (37).

Ciulla (2006) addresses the issue of ethics related to leadership, particularly, responsible or principled leadership: the examination of right, wrong, good, evil, virtue, duty, obligation, rights, and fairness. She argues that leaders are to be held to the same high standard of morality like everyone else in society. The reasonable expectation is that these leaders "will fail less than most people at meeting ethical standards, while pursuing and achieving the goals of their constituents." In other words, leaders must be more successful in keeping moral standards because "the price of their failure is greater than the ordinary person" (24). Her conclusion is that the study of leadership is the study of "what is good leadership"—what it ought to be and how to develop competent (effective) and morally responsible (ethical) leaders for today's society.

Rhode (2006) writes about the critical need for moral leadership in today's corporate world of business. In Rhode's book, the question of ethics dominates the entire discussion—what constitutes moral leadership; why moral leadership is ever so important today; why ethics pay; how do individuals, corporations, and contexts influence ethical conduct; and what strategies promote ethical and moral leadership.

Price (2006), writing insightfully about the ethics of authentic transformational leadership, points out that pseudo-transformational leaders may not be morally true to themselves and to those whom they lead when they practice favoritism, victimization, special interests, and end values such as racial or cultural superiority, submission, and survival of the fittest, as opposed to values of honesty, loyalty, fairness, justice, equality, and human rights. He asserts that: "the theory of transformational leadership underestimates the complexity of the moral psychology of leaders. . . . Such leaders fail to do what they should do, not because of self-interest, but because they think that these requirements are overridden by the other-regarding values to which they are committed" (9).

In using the metaphor of light and shadow, Johnson (2005, 9–19) highlights three ethical challenges or shadows facing leaders in our contemporary world: (1) the shadow of power, "[t]he more power we have, the more likely others will comply with our wishes" (10), which includes deceit, constraints, coercion, selfishness, inequity, cruelty, disregard, and deification; (2) the shadow of privilege, "[t]he greater the leader's power, generally, the greater the rewards he or she receives. . . . The link between power and privilege means that abuse of one generally leads to the abuse of the other" (p. 16); and (3) the shadow of deceit, which includes practices such as denying having knowledge that is in their possession, withholding information that followers need, using information solely for personal benefit, violating the privacy rights of followers, and releasing information to the wrong people. These three ethical challenges are interrelated and the problem common to all three is the abuse of power.

The Use and Abuse of Power

Various research papers have been written by several authors about the use and abuse of power; this research is included in an edited work by Annette Y. Lee-Chai and John A. Bargh (2001). This is an excellent collection of data that examines the psychological, social, and cultural dimensions of the use and abuse of power by individuals, groups, organizations, and governments in politics, business, and education in Western, European, and Asian cultures.

In their work titled "The Road to Hell: Good Intentions in the Face of Nonconscious Tendencies to Misuse Power," (Lee-Chai and Bargh 2001, 41–55) Bargh and Alvarez claim that abuse of power occurs at all levels of the power hierarchy. "From national governments to university academic departments, large corporations to local employee unions, individual power holders often use their officially sanctioned, legitimate power over others in illegitimate ways for personal and selfish gain" (p. 41). They cite two high costs of power abuse: (1) The organizational growth and potential are stunted when power holders abuse their positions for personal gains rather than the organization's; and (2) Abuse of power leads to overt or covert resistance and conflict from subordinates who feel that they have been treated unfairly or unjustly. Their research deals with those who unconsciously abuse their power, thinking at the conscious level that they are acting in an objective and fair-minded manner, and in the best interest of their subordinates (p. 45). There are two types of leaders who fall under this category: (1) one who has an automatic negative evaluation of the subordinate; and (2) one who has a mental concept of "having power" that is associated with one's important strivings and goal pursuits (pp. 46–47). The authors base their hypotheses on several researches carried out by various academics in the field of behavioral psychology (cf. pp. 46–49). They conclude that it is universally assumed that there is an innate need for power in the human psyche, but this does not quite explain why people abuse their power. The critical factor to consider is that individuals "differ in their important and self-defining goals—with some having self-centered and others more prosocial goals" (p. 53). Over time, these individual goals become automated, and these goals are pursued when they are in positions of authority over others without them even realizing that they are pursuing that goal in their situation.

Pratto and Walker (chapter 6: "Dominance in Disguise: Power, Beneficence, and Exploitation in Personal Relationships," 93–112) discuss how leaders disguise their abuse of power in personal relationships. The authors cited a study of national opinion data in the United States in 1994 by M. R. Jackman ("The Velvet Glove: Paternalism and Conflict in Gender, Class, and Race Relations." Berkeley, CA: University of California Press), which concluded that paternalistic ideologies that are disguised in velvet glove are more effective than bare iron fist, and that paternalism bears out in the form of inter-group attitudes with respect to class, race, and gender, with race being most controversial, and gender relations the most paternalistic.

According to Pratto and Walker, "people within a culture share understanding about how people ought to behave and use those understandings to justify or disapprove of people's actions and social practices," and that ideologies "help to create power differences and enable exploitation" (99). They summarize seven ways that ideologies can be used to justify or create an imbalance of power to enable exploitation to take place (102). (1) Certain ideologies lend themselves to discriminate power distance between one group over another without overtly demeaning the disadvantaged or elevating the advantaged. (2) Ideologies give power to those who are more in need than others who have lesser needs. (3) When ideologies of communion are used to shield differences in interests and needs, this deception can result in exploitation. (4) When ideologies that serve the powerful are used as general principles that apply equally to everyone, the less powerful are disadvantaged. (5) When dominants use ideologies to define the needs and wants of subordinates to serve the dominants' purpose, they not only practice exploitation but also justify it as the subordinates' wants. (6) Ideologies that describe people as having more or less power than they actually have can enable an exploitative arrangement to appear equitable or even make an exploiter seem exploited. (7) Ideologies that disguise control in affectionate and benevolent attitudes toward those they subordinate enable exploitation to go uncontested. Only the first ideological means of establishing power can be overt, while the other six ideological means "can aid exploitation, disguise inequalities in power, needs, or resources in the masks of equality, equal treatment, communalism, benevolence, and affection" (102–3).

Pratto and Walker coin the term, "parentalistic relationships,"—"according to the parental ideal, subordinates are succored" (p. 93). The authors point out that the critical difference between beneficent and exploitative parentalism is whether the dominant's power is used to prioritize the dominant's or the subordinate's needs (p. 110). The authors offer a few suggestions to prevent exploitative parentalism. (1) Prevent the dominant's needs to get ahead of the subordinates'. (2) Limit the power of the dominant over the subordinates. (3) Change the structural situations that enable exploitation and abuse of power. (4) Scrutinize the dominant's rhetoric and actions and match these against subordinates' needs and well-being.

In the following section, I propose that moral or ethical leadership based on virtue (good character) and deontological (principled) ethics is essential for today's leaders. Virtue and principle ethics are necessary as complementary systems for the leader to think, feel, and act morally or ethically. Two significant leadership theorists are presented: James MacGregor Burns (1978), *Leadership*, and Robert K. Greenleaf (1977), *Servant Leadership*. These two theories address the necessity to be virtuous leaders who think, feel, and act morally or ethically, and lead through serving others as servant leaders.

THE NORMATIVE THEORIES OF ETHICAL OR MORAL LEADERSHIP

"Normative leadership tells leaders how they ought to act. They are built on moral principles or norms but, unlike general ethical perspectives, deal directly with leader-follower relationships" (Johnson 2005, 157). Two prominent proponents of moral or ethical leadership are worthy of mention: James MacGregor Burn's *Transforming Leadership* and Robert Greenleaf's *Servant Leadership* (e.g., Cuilla 2004, 2006; Hitt 1990; Kellerman 2004; Johnson 2005; Kets de Vries and Miller 1997; Maak and Pless 2006; Price 2006; Rickards and Clark 2006).

James MacGregor Burns' Transforming Leadership (1978)

James MacGregor Burn's theory of transforming leadership is worthy to be considered normative for our consideration because it posits a set of moral assumptions about the relationship between leaders and followers. According to Price (2006), "Burn's conception of transforming leadership [is] the most influential normative conception of leadership in the literature" (9).

James MacGregor Burns serves as a political scientist at Williams College. His book, *Leadership* (1978) is a seminal research on political leadership. His theory on leadership is considered normative theory that describes the relationship between a leader and a follower in terms of shared values.

Burns defines "moral leadership" as one in which leaders and followers raise one another's perception and practice to higher levels of morality and motivation. In his work, Burns uses the terms *transforming leadership* and *transformational leadership*; however, he prefers the former to the latter. He defines transforming leadership: "when one or more persons *engage* with others in such a way that leaders and followers raise one another to higher levels of motivation and morality. . . . Such leadership ultimately becomes *moral* in that it raises the level of human conduct and aspiration of both the leader and the led, and thus it has transforming effect on both" (20).

His descriptive research on political leaders draws upon the works of Abraham Maslow's hierarchy of needs, Milton Rokeach's values development, and the moral development theories of Lawrence Kohlberg, Jean Piaget, Erik Erickson, and Alfred Adler.

Burns contends that moral leaders have to function and lead at higher levels of needs and values than those whom they are leading. Burns' theory is to raise the levels of conflicts and tensions in the value systems of the followers, and challenging them by raising their level of consciousness to act upon them.

Burns' seminal work on the lives and decision-making processes of political leaders raises two fundamental issues in leadership: how does one make ethical decisions, and how does one use power in the office of authority? Burns' theory of transforming or good leadership seeks to hold leaders accountable for both their private and public lives.

In discussing the concepts of transactional leadership and transformational leadership, he makes the distinction between the two concepts with the understanding of modal and end values that constitute good leadership. In essence, Burns is asking the question: Does whatever means one employs justify the end? Transactional leadership is one of mutual exchange of lower needs, which he calls modal values. Things like responsibility, fairness, honesty, and promises that the leader and follower adhere to, are exchanged as means to an agreed end. On the other hand, transforming leadership deals with higher end values such as liberty, justice, and equality. Burns believes that transforming leaders raise the levels of morality in their followers to become transforming leaders themselves as moral agents of value change.

In a very insightful article on ethics and authentic transformational leadership, Terry Price (2006) discusses the possibility that "the theory of transformational leadership underestimates the complexity of the moral psychology of leaders . . . [and] leadership can induce and maintain a leader's belief that he is somehow excepted from moral requirements" that apply to others (124–25). Drawing from MacGregor Burns' moral treatise, *Leadership*, Price claims that "[it] can be read as an argument about the kinds of selves to which leaders should be true" (124). Price goes on to typify three versions of pseudo-transformational leaderships, namely, incontinent, base, and opportunistic, and assigns their ethical failures to the problems of will, not to the problems of belief and knowledge. For Burns, the test of an authentic transforming leader is one who adheres to values of morality and is willing "to apply standards to oneself as well as to others" (75).

Yukl (2002) summarizes Burns' transforming leadership: "Thus, transforming leadership involves not only the moral elevation of individual followers, but also collective efforts to accomplish social reforms. In the process, both the leader and followers will be changed. They will begin to consider not only what is good for themselves, but also what will benefit larger collectivities such as their organization, community, and nation" (403).

Robert Greenleaf's Servant Leadership: Putting the Interests of the Followers First

"Greenleaf's idea of servant leadership (1977/2002) has been the second most influential, explicitly normative concept of leadership aside from Burns' idea of transforming leadership (1978, 2003). What makes it so appealing for so many scholars and, particularly, practitioners, is the striking idea that leadership is not about the grandiosity of a leader but about those he or she serves" (Maak and Pless 2006, 45).

Robert Greenleaf (1977) spent forty years in research, development, and education at AT&T and twenty-five years as an organizational consultant. He first coined the term "servant leader" in the early 1970s to describe a philosophy of leadership where the interests of the followers are placed first in the leader's mind and heart.

Greenleaf's inspiration came from the novel *The Journey to the East*, by Hermann Hesse (1956). The story is about a group of travelers on a mystical and spiritual journey to the East. On the journey a servant named Leo carries the bags and does all the chores that travelers do. Leo has a great influence on the travelers with him. Leo is the one who keeps the group together merrily along the way until one day when he disappears from the scene. The group disintegrates and abandons the journey to the East. Without Leo the group cannot hold themselves together to move ahead and complete the journey. The concept of servant leadership as Hermann Hesse (1956) described it, is felt and discovered only after the servant leader is absent: "It was the absence of the servant Leo which revealed to us, suddenly and terribly, the extent of the dissention and the perplexities which shattered our hitherto apparent complex unity. . . . Hardly had Leo left us, when faith and concord amongst us was at an end; it was as if the life-blood of our group flowed away from the invisible wound" (112–13).

Later in the book the main character Hermann Hesse (HH), discovers that the servant, Leo, is actually the leader of the group. "The simple but radical shift in emphasis is from followers serving leaders to leaders serving followers" (Ciulla 1998, 17).

The fundamental questions to ask about servant leadership are as follows: "Do those served grow as persons? Do they, while being served, become healthier, wiser, freer, more autonomous, more likely themselves to become servants?" (Greenleaf, 13–14). Servant leadership has many adherents among noted writers, thinkers, and leaders (Spears 1995) such as Max Depree, Peter Senge, Peter Block, Walter Wright (cf. Banks and Ledbetter 2004, 107–12).

Larry Spears, the executive director of the Robert K. Greenleaf Center for Leadership (Indianapolis), names ten characteristics (from the writings of Greenleaf) of the servant leader. These are the abilities to listen well, to have empathy, to heal, to have awareness of the reality on the ground, to persuade as opposed to coerce, to have positional authority, to conceptualize, to exercise foresight, to commit to the growth of people, and to commit to the building of community (Spears 1994, 153-59).

Observing Christian leadership and comparing it to what Greenleaf has insisted—"that a leader is a servant first and only in the wake of that service is a leader"—Banks and Ledbetter (2004) make a startling discovery about Christian leaders: "[M]any people in authority place the main emphasis on the second word rather than the first" (110). In their leadership posture, these leaders still maintain command and control, and "have co-opted the language of servant leadership for their own agendas and purposes. Sad to say, this has often been the case in the church and in many religious organizations" (110).

According to Johnson (2005), there are four key related concepts that hold the practice of servant leadership together: (1) Stewardship—"as agents of followers who entrust them with special duties and opportunities for a limited time"; (2) Obligation—"Servant leaders take their obligations or responsibilities seriously"; (3) Partnership—"Servant leaders view followers as partners not subordinates"; and (4) Elevating purpose—"Seeking to fulfill a high moral purpose, and understanding the role one plays in the process, makes work more meaningful to leaders and followers" (173–75). Johnson concludes that there are also four strengths in the exercise of leadership, namely, altruism, simplicity, self-awareness, and moral sensitivity (175–76).

SUMMARY

Based on social-science-leadership theories and power-influence theories, CCL manifests unethical leadership in its transactional use of positional, coercive, and reward power bases, which breeds compliant and uncritical followers as opposed to ethical leadership (of theorists Burns and Greenleaf) which advocate virtue (character) and deontological (principled) ethics.

Two prominent power-influence theories, namely the social power approach (five power bases) and social exchange approach (transactional and transformational leadership), help us understand the mechanics of leadership practices in the exercise of power and authority, and their effects on followership.

Based on the social power-bases approach of French and Raven's (1959), CCL primarily uses positional power bases (legitimate, coercive, and reward) in the exercise of paternalistic authority. The use of such power bases leads to compliant followership. Using Kelley's (1992) construct on followership styles, CCL produce followers who are passive, conformist, uncritical in thinking, and pragmatic for self-serving reasons; and alienated followers.

Based on the social exchange approach to leadership, in Kanungo and Mendoca's (1996) study of leadership influence processes, we learn about how the ethical implications of CCL elicit compliant behavior. CCL's transactional use of coercive, legal, and reward power bases is characteristic of unethical leadership.

Two other studies on the harmful effects of the abuse of power and authority—unconscious tendencies and dominance, in disguise—reveal the self-centeredness of the leader in the former, and the paternalistic tendencies of the leader in the latter.

Moral or ethical leadership based on virtue (good character) and deontological (principled) ethics is essential for today's leaders. Two significant leadership theorists are presented: James MacGregor Burns (1978), *Leadership* and Robert K. Greenleaf (1977), *Servant Leadership*.

These two theories address the necessity to be virtuous leaders who think, feel, and act morally or ethically, and who lead their followers with a spirit of servanthood.

5

Moral Formation and Servanthood as Counter-Cultural Paradigm for Christian Leaders

IN A VERY INSIGHTFUL article in *Christianity Today* (June 2008), Taylor and McCloskey ask the question, "How to Pick a President: Why Virtue Trumps Policy" (22–28). They argue as to why virtue is of utmost importance when it comes to selecting a president for the United States. Refuting the camp that believes that competence is the sole determinant for presidential selection, Taylor and McCloskey assert that "competence without virtue is poisonous. . . . [B]eing virtuous is, in itself, an expression of competence . . . [and] a lack of virtue in a leader is a sign of incompetence and grounds enough for rejecting that leadership" (24). Virtue refers to a person's good character traits and high moral standards and is vital in a leader. "Virtue is a suite of values-soaked abilities that in active combination form a person's character and give shape to a life. Our choices and actions both reveal and reinforce our character. You cannot judge whether a person will be a good leader—a good President—without knowing and evaluating his or her character—how life has stamped or marked them" (24).

The basic requirement of Christian leaders is to be morally formed in both character and conduct, as taught in Scriptures. Rae provides insight on the relationship between the scriptural and ethical perspectives on the subject of moral character formation. Rae (2000) coherently argues that deontological ethics, which places emphasis on principles in which actions (or character, or even intentions), are inherently right or wrong predominates New Testament ethics (28). Rae views virtue ethics as *complementary* to deontological ethics. For the Christian, moral virtues have an intrinsic value in that the virtues not only involves the right action but also the right motive and attitude. "Virtues are a constitutive element of the good life and especially of being like Christ. Thus, a complementary view of virtues and principles would appear to be more consistent with Scripture. Perhaps virtues are even logically prior to principles, insofar as God's character expresses itself in virtues, and moral rules and principles then are those that are consistent with the outworking of God's virtues" (99–100).

In this chapter I propose the servanthood model, exemplified by Jesus Christ, as the counter-cultural paradigm for Christian leaders in relation to the use of power and authority in leadership. Servanthood is both a character-forming ethic (virtue) as well as a biblical- or theological-principled ethic (deontological) for the Christian leader who leads *not* from a posture of position, power, or prestige, but from a posture of Christlike humility—serving the interests of others over self preservation.

Contemporary (or Practiced) Confucian Leadership has been a source of tension in Christian ministry among Asians in Asia as well as Asian Americans in the North American context. Its values predispose Christian leaders toward paternalistic authoritarianism resembling the nine manifestations of power usage as described in chapter 3. These manifestations of power, or authority, are also known as coercive and reward power bases in the literature of power and influence theories (cf. discussions in chapter 4).

Asian Christian leaders in East Asia and Southeast Asia have deplored such use of paternalistic authoritarianism in Christian leadership. Eun Seung Lee in his doctoral dissertation (2004) surveyed his sample respondents (twenty-three top scoring Korean senior pastors who were identified as transformational) concerning what a transformational pastor looked like in a Korean church context. He found among other conclusions, "Most respondents consciously rejected Confucian leadership style because of its characteristics of authoritarian attitudes, sectarian mindset, male superiority, non-biblical high priest theology" (176).

Citing research in master and doctoral theses (Pak 1988; Son 2000; Chin 2001), Lee classified three "authoritarian and vertical leadership" styles adopted by the Korean society in general—the king, the *Sunbi* (scholar/mentor), and the father (68). These three models have pervaded the Korean culture. All three models command "absolute authority" from the ruled, the people, and the offspring. Pastors behave like kings, as if their authority was mandated from heaven, and they serve with the assumption of "positional power" endowed from above regardless of their inability to command the respect of the congregation. "When authoritarian leadership and positional power are practiced, it is easy for the leadership style to become dominant and abusive and is not beneficial to the followers" (Lee, 71).

"The future of Korean church may need a healthy, ethical, and biblically sound leadership model that inspires, empowers, . . . providing some solutions for the problematic leadership issues in today's Korean church" (74).

In the light of the pervasive Confucian values in the Singapore culture, Esther Chelliah, in her doctoral dissertation (2001), examined these values that Singapore Methodist (English speaking) pastors have embraced in their pastoral leadership.

> Singapore's Confucian worldview is a product of worldly wisdom. It is a secular humanistic culture of pragmatism that promotes virtue not truth. Behavior not belief is critical in this worldview. Fulfilling duty according to one's status in the social hierarchy of relationships is central. Conceptual truth has little relevance. In the biblical worldview belief determines behavior. All virtues emanate from God's truth. Truth in one's being results in the doing, but the Confucian value of virtue and duty encourage a culture of doing that defines humans. People are valued for what they can produce, not who they are. The doing comes forth from the being and not the other way round. The culture of being fosters relationships and produces psychologically healthy persons where human worth is not determined by one's profession or occupation. The culture of doing reduces the person to a statistic, and economic resource, and is violent to the human psyche. The culture of doing values everything from a utilitarian pragmatic perspective that reduces the worth of a person to an economic resource and a demographic statistic.
>
> The Methodist philosophy of leadership has been influenced by Confucian cultural values of leadership. Therefore, it is not able to overcome the human tendencies and weaknesses found in its values of leadership. Both uphold values of virtue, hierarchy, authority, and compliance. Both affirmed the centralization of power in leadership and perpetuated structures that would sustain it. . . .

> Though the Methodist Church has its origins in the Spirit of God, in its outworking it tends to reflect secular values of leadership.
>
> Traditions that do not have their source in the Spirit of God and the Scriptures are to be held lightly in the life of the church, leadership, and ministry. Norms of culture must be evaluated in the light of the biblical worldview. (235–36)

Keith Hinton (1992), in his analysis of Christian leadership and authority among churches in Singapore, made these claims:

> The traditional pattern of Chinese authority has been characterized by autocratic direction, hierarchy, respect for and rule by elders. Leadership has been based on ascription rather than achievement, and marked by the repetition of past ways. The new generation has been influenced by a new set of values with more emphasis on democratic patterns, free, creative thinking, and often a degree of orientation to the future and change that the "new" tends to expected to be better than the old. The old and the new clash, with the old *ruling* rather than *leading*, *forcing* its goals on members in military manner rather than *selling* them. Responsibility is not easily delegated, and so little room is left for initiative in the tasks allotted to rank and file. In spite of the resentment of the young towards this style of leadership and despite all the western influences to which they are exposed, it is always surprising how younger Chinese quickly revert to traditional Chinese pattern when they themselves become leader, tending to become equally as autocratic as their forebears. (italics author's, 52)

Given the prevalence of the practice of CCL among leaders who are in Christian ministry in Confucian societies, the teachings of Jesus Christ on character virtues (Matt 5:3–12, 17–48) and on servanthood (Matt 20:20–28) serve as pivotal values in the face of the challenge of CCL practices, particularly in the misuse of power and authority.

ETHICAL TEACHINGS OF JESUS CHRIST (MATT 5)

The teachings of Jesus, recorded in the Gospel of Matthew chapters 5 to 7, are commonly referred to as the Sermon on the Mount (SOTM). The SOTM serves as the moral vision for the Christian leader and embodies character and deontological ethics. It addresses vertical relationship with God (piety) and relationships with each other (ethical practice or ethics) (cf. Stott 1978). The former can be found in Matthew 5:3–6, 33;

6:1–18, 33; 7:7–11. The latter can be found in Matthew 5:21–26, 27–30, 38–48; 7:1–6.

The purpose of the SOTM is to challenge people with the demands of discipleship and to give instructions to those who follow Jesus as their Master. The eight Beatitudes (5:3–12) and the two metaphors of salt and light (5:13–16) lay the foundation and introduce the SOTM. Matthew 5:17–20, particularly verse 20, gives the crux to the matter—the "greater righteousness" required of Jesus' followers. There are four large teaching units within the SOTM: 5:21–48; 6:1–18; 6:19–34; 7:1–12. Each of these four large units of thought confronts the establishment of Jesus' day. Matthew 5:21–48 challenges the reader to an inward transformation of heart, as opposed to the religiosity of keeping the law without the spirit of the law. Matthew 6:1–18 challenges the establishment to examine their motives in three acts of piety—giving, prayer, and fasting. Matthew 6:19–34 challenges the anxious and covetous heart and calls for radical trust in the goodness and generosity of God for his own. Matthew 7:1–12 challenges the judgmental spirit that fails to examine oneself before judging another.

For the purpose of this study, I will focus on Matthew 5:3–12 and Matthew 5:17–48 for insights on ethical instructions. The Beatitudes (Matt 5:3–12) "emphasize eight principal marks of Christian character and conduct in relation to God and to men" (Stott 1978, 24). The six ethical test cases (Matt 5:17–48) summon the Christian to a "greater righteousness" (Matt 5:20), which is a "deep inward righteousness of the heart where the Holy Spirit has written God's law" (123).

The Significance of the Sermon on the Mount as Moral Foundation for the Christian Disciple/Leader

Moral formation is foundational for Christian leadership. Moral formation is developed through our understanding of philosophical ethical systems of virtue and deontological ethics. "Ethics is about the good (that is, what values and virtues we should cultivate) and about the right (that is, what our moral duties may be)" (Holmes 1984, 10). The Sermon on the Mount emphasizes virtue ethics and what Rae (2000) refers to as a "reinterpreted deontology" (biblical principles for character or actions). This reinterpreted deontology gives critical attention to principles that lead to moral behavior, both in terms of motivation and character formation (cf. Hollinger 2002, 166–73).

The Sermon on the Mount emphasizes the ethic of love for God and for people (Matt 5–7). It emphasizes the ethic of virtue which is an inner righteousness, as opposed to outward conformity to rules and regulations (Matt 5:20, 17–48; cf. Matt 5:15, 23). "Righteousness is not just a matter of right conduct but a matter of the heart, not just a question of what I value and what I do, but of the kind of person I am at the core of my being" (Holmes 1991, 58). Elaborating on the call to righteousness in the SOTM, Hagner (2007) affirms:

> The righteousness of the new community is of radical character. The Sermon on the Mount is its blueprint. Those who will manifest it are described as "the salt to the earth" and "the light to the world" (5:13). They are learning to deal not merely with their actions . . . but also with their thoughts, with their heart, with their innermost being. They are faithful; their word is as good as gold. Far from being vengeful, they are loving and good, even towards their enemies. They are not hypocrites, playacting, pretending to be something they are not. Their piety is more private than public. They are forgiving of others, just as they have experienced God's forgiveness. They are not materialistic. They are not anxious, but place their trust in God's provision for them. They make the kingdom of God their priority. They are not judgmental. They act towards others as they would like others to act towards them. They are serious about the call to righteousness. (49–50)

In the broader context of New Testament theology, the foundation for moral formation in the Christian disciple/leader must go hand in hand with a yielding to the power of the Holy Spirit for life transformation (John 13–17; Rom 6–8; 2 Cor 3:18; Gal 5:16, 22–23).

For the Christian, virtues precede principles insofar as God's holy character is concerned, and moral-biblical principles are the consistent representation of the outworking of God's virtues in action. Such a disciple/leader models Christ and seeks to live under the power of the indwelling Holy Spirit, as opposed to acts of the human flesh (Gal 5:22–23 vs. Gal 5:19–21; cf. Mark 7:20–23; 1 Cor 6:9–10). This is the biblical concept of sanctification.

The Beatitudes—Matthew 5:3–12

Doriani (2006) argues that the Beatitudes are "kingdom virtues" that "do more than describe a disciple; they also describe Jesus, the master" (15). Virtues are qualities that make up a person's character (Stassen and Gushee 2003, 32). The Beatitudes form the foundational virtues for the Christian follower or leader. Matthew 5:3–12 prescribes a path toward character formation that seeks to relate to God, and then to others. The first three beatitudes demonstrate the disciple's spiritual need for God (v. 3 "poor in spirit," v. 4 "mourn," v. 5 "meek"); these spiritual needs will be met in the fourth beatitude in verse 6 ("they will be filled"); and as a result of being filled and satisfied, they will demonstrate virtues of mercy (v. 7), purity (v 8), and peacemaking (v. 9).

Each beatitude begins with a pronouncement of blessing ("blessed") followed by a statement of the recipient of the blessing. With each pronouncement, the *hoti*—"for" or "because"—clause is used, giving the reason for the pronouncement of each blessing. The English word "blessed" in Greek is *makarios*. Some translations have translated the Greek word to mean "happy," which "tends to trivialize the meaning by simply suggesting a temporary emotional or circumstantial state" (Wilkins 2004, 204). To be "blessed" by God means "to be approved, to find approval" (Carson 1978, 16) from him who gives man life. When we are blessed by God, we are "in a happy state"—we are joyful, even when our circumstances and situations may sometimes dictate otherwise. Matthew records eight such "blessings."

Matthew 5:3. Blessed are the poor in spirit, for theirs is the kingdom of heaven. Being "poor in spirit" refers to "the acknowledgement of one's spiritual powerlessness and bankruptcy apart from Christ" (Blomberg 1992, 98). It is the opposite of human pride and self-righteousness. Those who are "poor in spirit" recognize that they have no merit of their own before God, and therefore have no basis for boasting or arrogance.

Matthew 5:4. Blessed are those who mourn, for they will be comforted. The mourning here refers to grieving over sin. The second beatitude follows the first in that those who recognize their own unworthiness before God ("poor in spirit") confess their wrong doings and turn away from their sins. In their remorse, confession, and repentance, God comforts them.

Matthew 5:5. Blessed are the meek, for they will inherit the earth. The "meek" in this context refers to those who are gentle and self-controlled. Meekness as a character trait is the opposite of ambition and envy. It follows that those who are "poor in spirit," would "mourn" over their sins, and realizing their spiritual poverty, they would be humble and gentle in spirit. They will receive their reward, "for they will inherit the earth" (cf. Ps 37:11).

Matthew 5:6. Blessed are those who hunger and thirst for righteousness, for they will be filled. "Righteousness" in the context of the SOTM refers to a number of things. It includes (1) "justice" for those who have been bullied; (2) personal ethical righteousness that is free from the clutches of sin; (3) personal standing before God based on Christ's redemptive act; (4) hope of a future kingdom to come; and (5) vindication of those who have been treated unjustly (Carson 1984, 134; Talbert 2004, 52; Wilkins 2004, 206). For disciples who truly long for these various forms of righteousness, the promise is that they will be filled. Their desire (thirst and hunger) for God's righteousness (both present and future) issues out of a heart that acknowledges its own spiritual impoverishment, in contrast to the attitude of self-righteousness and self-sufficiency. The disciple who knows and recognizes a deep need to be dependent upon God, hungers and thirsts for God's righteousness, and is satisfied by God.

Matthew 5:7. Blessed are the merciful, for they will be shown mercy. The "merciful" refers to the disciple who offers a forgiving heart toward the guilty, and a compassionate heart toward the suffering and needy (Carson 1984, 134). It is a reflection of God's heart to his people (e.g., Exod 34:6). The "merciful" is the disciple who is gentle, patient, and kind. The disciple extends mercy to those who do not deserve it, just as God in His mercy relates mercifully to all people who are undeserving of his mercy. The reward for the merciful is that they will be shown mercy by God. The parable of the unmerciful servant who had been shown mercy (Matt 18:33) is a clear illustration of what a disciple ought *not* to follow.

Matthew 5:8. Blessed are the pure in heart, for they will see God. The sixth beatitude refers to "moral uprightness" as opposed to ritual cleanliness, as the Pharisees emphasize (Blomberg 1992, 100). Purity of heart is *not* sinless perfection before God and others, but it is a continuous process of drawing near to God in confession and repentance. Purity consists of two aspects—"inner moral purity" and "singlemindedness"—complementing each other in the life of a disciple. Having a pure heart is the antithesis to hypocrisy (cf. Matt 6:1–18) (Carson 1984, 134–35). Those whose hearts are pure will be rewarded—"they will see God." This has an eschatological hope (Rev 22:4); for the first hearers of this beatitude, they are rewarded with the presence of Jesus as Immanuel (Matt 1:23).

Matthew 5:9. Blessed are the peacemakers, for they will be called sons of God. The seventh beatitude refers to those who work toward *shalom* (Old Testament word for peace; New Testament word is *eirene*) and who reconcile others to God and to one another. They will be known as "sons of God," as they reflect the character of God. True disciples are called to be reconciled to one another (Matt 5:23–24), to love even their enemies, to pray for those who persecute them (5:43–45), and to bring others to God on behalf of Jesus Christ, the Supreme Peacemaker (Eph 2:11–17) who reconciles man to God.

Matthew 5:10–12. Blessed are those who are persecuted because of righteousness, for theirs is the kingdom of heaven. Blessed are you when people insult you, persecute you and falsely say all kinds of evil against you because of me. Rejoice and be glad, because great is your reward in heaven, for in the same way they persecuted the prophets who were before you. Those who exhibit the virtues of the first seven beatitudes will be persecuted. The kind of persecution that is blessed of God has to do with a different lifestyle and conduct that stems from values that are akin to Jesus and his teachings. Disciples should "rejoice" when they are persecuted because (1) the prophets of the Old Testament suffered for the sake of righteousness; and (2) there is a future reward awaiting those who suffer persecution for righteousness.

Six Ethical Test-Cases—Matthew 5:17–48

According to Talbert (2000), the gospel writer Matthew highlighted the deficient understanding of righteousness of the Pharisees, compared to the surpassing righteousness that Jesus spoke about in Matthew 5:17–20 (64). Matthew pointed out that (1) The Pharisees rely on their ascribed status instead of obeying the will of God; they do not practice what they teach (Matt 23:3); (2) They major on the minor points and minor on the major points (23:23–24); (3) They seek human approval over God's (23:5, 27–28); (4) They evade the true intent of the Law (23:16–22; 15:1–9). They are ceremonially cleansed without, but decaying within (23:25).

The Pharisees and the teachers of the law adhered strictly to outward standards of religiosity, e.g., in fasting, tithing, and praying, according to the rules that they had instituted as law. However, Jesus countered their faulty thinking with the key verse in 5:20: "For I tell you that unless your righteousness surpasses that of the Pharisees and the teachers of the law, you will certainly not enter the kingdom of heaven." In Matthew 5:17–48, Jesus is calling his disciples to an inner righteousness, as opposed to outer righteousness based on rules and regulations. Using six case studies, Jesus lays down the New Testament ethic of virtue (character) and deontology (principle) that flow from a life of inner righteousness.

Murder (5:21–26). Here Jesus refers to the sixth commandment of the Decalogue—"you shall not murder" (Exod 20:13). "Murder" encompasses the idea of intentionality of taking someone's physical life, but excludes self-defense, wars decreed by Yahweh, or lawful capital punishment. Jesus, in his argument, begins with "But I tell you—" (v. 22) and cites three mannerisms (all referring to the harboring of wrath in the heart) that are deserving of punishment. The person who manifests any one of these three "heart harboring" mannerisms is just as guilty of "murder." The first "heart harboring" mannerism is anger: "But I tell you that anyone who is angry with his brother will be subject to judgment" (v. 22). The source of "murder" is a heart that is inappropriately angry at someone (cf. 1 John 3:15). The second mannerism is to call a fellow disciple ("brother") *raca*, an Aramaic swear-word implying that the person is "empty headed" (Blomberg 1992, 107). The third mannerism is to call someone "You fool!" (v. 22). This name calling shows contempt for another person. In elaborating the seriousness of expressions or mannerisms of anger, Jesus provides the higher righteousness principle, i.e., the need to be reconciled with your brother (vv. 23–24) and your adversary (25–26).

In this antithesis, Jesus challenges the reading of the law's command, "Do not murder." It is not the physical act of murder that is in question but relationships between people. Inappropriate anger, which leads to broken relationships, is equivalent to murder. It is the inner issue of the heart that needs addressing: "the [first] antithesis aims to shape the disciple's character in the direction of concern for the health and wholeness of relationships among God's people" (Talbert 2004, 71).

Adultery (5:27–30). In this second antithesis, Jesus raises the issue of adultery—the seventh commandment in the Decalogue (Exod

20:14)—and alludes to the tenth commandment regarding covetousness (Exod 20:17). Adultery refers to an illicit sexual relationship between a married person and someone other than his or her lawfully married spouse.

Jesus' use of the word "lust" (5:28) refers to the same Greek word that is sometimes translated as "coveting." Lust is the desire in a person's heart to covet someone, to possess that person or to have an immoral relationship with that person. The person who lusts has already committed adultery in God's eyes. The severity of lust is that it is adultery that has taken root in the heart. It has to be dealt with quickly and radically (vv. 29–30).

Divorce (5:31–32). In this third antithesis, Jesus defends the sanctity of marriage by referring to Moses' command in Deuteronomy 24:1. This command from God through Moses serves three purposes: (1) To prevent marriage from being defiled by acts of indecency; (2) to protect the wife from being unfairly abused by the arbitrary treatment of the husband; and (3) to prove the legitimate status of the divorced wife that she was not a harlot or adulteress (Wilkins 2004, 246).

In Jesus' time, the legitimacy of divorce had become a very rule-based, matter-of-fact procedure that allowed the husband to discard the wife whenever he was displeased with her for any reason that might allude to indecency, as stated in Deuteronomy 24:1–4. To counter the culture of his day, Jesus states that divorce is tantamount to adultery because divorce makes the wife an adulteress when she remarries.

Jesus upholds the permanency of the marriage ideal, as God intended for a married couple (Gen 2:24). However, divorce is permitted not on frivolous grounds, but only "if all attempts at reconciliation have failed because . . . adultery has already undermined one of the most fundamental elements of a marriage—sexual exclusivity" (Blomberg 1992, 110–11). Jesus is more concerned about protecting the unoffending partner and to preserve the sanctity of the marriage vows from becoming an excuse for frivolous divorces to take place.

Oath (5:33–37). The fourth antithesis deals with the Old Testament concept concerning oath. Outside of the Decalogue, the law demands that a person honors what has been sworn or whatever commitment has been made to another (Lev 19:12; Num 30:2). In Jesus' day, there were those who differentiated various kinds of vows or oaths, and if these were not made in the name of the Lord, the vow or oath was not binding. However,

Jesus countered this by saying that his disciples should not make any vow or swear at all.

Jesus knew the complexity and duplicity of the human heart (cf. Jer 17:9) and recognized that when people made vows or oaths, they did so to hide something or to deceive someone. The disciple of Jesus should be a person of integrity and honor; whatever he or she says is absolutely dependable and trustworthy.

Retaliation (5:38–42). In the fifth antithesis, Jesus takes issue with those who use the law of retaliation (*lex talionis*) to justify revenge. In Deuteronomy 19:20–21; Exodus 21:23–25; Leviticus 24:18–20, Moses provides in the law the right to justice and retribution against evil and evil doers in the community. The law of retaliation was to be enacted by the civil courts to protect the public and punish the offenders of evil acts; it was not meant to be used by any individual. In fact, Leviticus 19:18 encouraged the people of God to pursue love.

During Jesus' time, due to the Roman occupation and control over the Jews, injustices and chaos were the order of the day and hence personal revenge and retaliation became acceptable practices. Since the commoner could not be guaranteed justice from the Roman empire, people began to look out for themselves rather than look for the higher purpose of love for their neighbor. Jesus countered this prevailing thought. Disciples who are abused and taken advantage of should not think of retaliation as an option. Instead, "they must think of ways to advance the kingdom of heaven and its influence on earth" (Wilkins 2004, 249). Jesus uses four illustrations to make himself understood. (1) When disciples are insulted publicly, they do not retaliate with evil, but with good (cf. Rom 12:19–21; 1 Thess 5:15). (2) When they are sued in court for their tunic, they must give their cloak as well. (3) When they are required by someone to "go one mile" as in military operations, they should offer to go two miles. (4) When someone comes to them for help, even though the former is undeserving of help or assistance, the disciples are to give freely without thought of repayment.

Enemy-Love (5:43–48) The sixth antithesis, "Love your neighbor," comes from Leviticus 19:18, but "hate your enemy" is not found anywhere in the Old Testament. Jesus tells his listeners to "love your enemies and pray for those who persecute you" (5:44). God hates evil but loves people, and his purpose is to reconcile people to him and to one another. His argument is built upon God's common grace upon mankind—God offers sun and rain to all of his creation; everyone, whether good or evil, comes under his providential care. Christ's disciples are to love even their enemies, otherwise they will be no different from tax collectors and pagans—people who look out for their own interests.

The sixth antithesis ends with verse 48: "Be perfect . . . as your heavenly Father is perfect." The word "perfect" may be better translated as "mature, whole." It connotes the idea of loving our enemies without limits—to become more like Christ (cf. 1 John 4:16) (Blomberg 1992, 114). The true test of disciples of Christ is whether they love those who hate, mistreat, or persecute them. Jesus' followers, who are able to love and greet their enemies and pray for their persecutors, demonstrate that they are growing in conformity to the likeness of their Heavenly Father (v. 45).

The six antitheses reinforced Jesus' teaching that inner righteousness in the heart of a person matters more than external conformity to laws and regulations. The condition of the heart—one's thoughts, motives, and attitudes—is the state of one's moral being and determines one's external behaviors. Hence, while his listeners were exhorted to pursue godly virtues, Jesus also cautioned against opposing mindsets, attitudes, and practices. In the context of the gospel of Matthew, these are represented in the persons of the Pharisees and scribes.

In Matthew 23, Jesus gave a scathing denunciation of the values and practices of the Pharisees and scribes. His denunciation is instructive and relevant, in the light of the discussion on Contemporary Confucian Leadership in our study. Looking at the values and practices of the authoritarian stance of CCL (see also ch. 3; Table 3.1, p. 30), we can identify some similar traits for which Jesus rebuked the Pharisees and scribes—legalism, hypocrisy, exploitation. Wilkins (2004) commented: "[M]any of the criticisms that Jesus lodges against the Pharisees can also be lodged against us. This is especially true of Christian leaders: . . . pride, public showmanship, one-upmanship, bullheadedness, politicizing of one's position, and of course, hypocrisy" (761).

The Pharisees "were members of the sect that was committed to fulfilling the demands of the Old Testament through their elaborate oral tradition" (Wilkins 2004, 231). However, their morality was questionable. Equating religious performance as acceptance before God, they exhibited self-righteousness. Jesus pointed out that this would not gain them entrance into the kingdom of heaven (Matt 5:20).

Jesus' criticism against the Pharisees in Matthew 23:1–12 confronts the unethical and immoral practices of legalism, hypocrisy, and exploitation of the leadership, not only during his day but in any age. Wilkins succinctly points out from the text that demanding legalistic performance from others abuses God's authority (vv. 1–4); pretentious public display of piety misrepresents God's authority (vv. 5–7); and exploiting titles and positions usurps God's authority (vv. 8–10) (Wilkins, 762). Concern for positions and prominence in leadership is faulty thinking (vv. 11–12; cf. Matt 20:26–27).

Conversely, Wilkins offers four positive lessons for Christian leaders: live by example of God's message of grace (23:1–4); earn respect and honor, do not demand them (23:5–7); wear titles lightly (23:8–10); and serve God's people to empower them to advance the kingdom of God (23:11–12) (763–64).

Summary of Ethical Teachings

The Sermon on the Mount serves as the moral vision for the Christian leader who aspires to live a godly life and lead in a godly fashion. The leader's character and conduct adheres to the ethical teachings of Jesus Christ. Character formation, based on virtue and deontological ethics, is foundational for the Christian disciple or leader. In Matthew 5, true discipleship calls for a transformation of heart that gives rise to external habits and patterns of living. Disciples who look to God are spiritually poor, sin mourners, humble, God-righteousness seekers, merciful, pure, peace-making, and willing to be persecuted for God-righteousness. Their inner righteousness confronts them to deal with ethical issues from the heart and not merely conform to rules and regulations. The difference in inner response and outer conformity can be seen in the six ethical cases of murder, adultery, divorce, oath, retaliation, and enemy-love.

Christian leaders lead by way of a grace-based relationship with followers, as opposed to a rule-based relationship of paternalistic authoritarianism, which hinges on legalism, hypocrisy, and exploitation. A grace-based relationship is built upon the virtues of being. Such a person relates to others from an inner moral core that is righteous (Matt 5:6), merciful (Matt 5:7), peaceable (Matt 5:9), conciliatory (Matt 5:21–26), non-retaliatory (Matt 5:38–42), and shows love even to enemies (Matt 5:43–48).

The Beatitudes are not meant as imperatives to follow in order to gain God's approval, but they remain as goals that the true disciple of Christ would hope to reach through the transforming power of the Holy Spirit. Jesus' teachings on virtues in the Beatitudes and the SOTM are what other New Testament biblical writers had written about concerning sanctification through the work of the Holy Spirit (e.g., Col 3:12–17; Phil 2:2–3; Eph 4:2–3, 32; Gal 5:22–23; Rom 14:17; 15:4–5; 2 Cor 6:4–10; 1 Tim 4:12; 6:11; 2 Tim 2:22; 3:10; 1 Pet 3:8; and 2 Pet 1:5–7; see also comparison charts by Stassen and Gushee 2003, 48–51).

Many Christian writers who write about Christian leadership refer to the model of servant leader as exemplified by Jesus Christ, particularly as shown from the Gospel accounts found in Matthew 20:20–28, Mark 10:35–45, and Luke 22:24–30 (e.g., Agee 2001; Banks and Ledbetter 2004; Beadles 2000; Blanchard 2005; Block 2005; Carter 1997; Clarke 2000; De Pree 1997, 1989; Elmer 2006; Engstrom 1976; Estep 2005; Ford 1991; Hutchison 2009; Hybels 2002; Issler 2001; Malphurs 2003; Marshall 1991; Means 1989; Miller 1995; Nouwen 1991; Porter 2000; Rardin 2001; Rinehart 1998; Sanders 1994; Shaw 2006; Tan 2006; Ward 1996; Wilkes 1998; Wilkins 2004).

In the following section, I propose that the servanthood ethic of Jesus Christ (Matt 20:20–28) as taught and demonstrated by Jesus Christ, presents a counter-cultural paradigm for Christian leadership that is virtuous and principled. In the prevailing culture of shame and honor, patronage, and preferential treatment based on kinship, greatness is measured in terms of position, power, and prestige. However, for the leader in Christian ministry, Christlike humility is the normative pattern for Christian leadership.

THE SERVANTHOOD ETHIC OF JESUS CHRIST AS COUNTER-CULTURAL PARADIGM FOR CHRISTIAN LEADERSHIP

Hutchison (2009) argues that it must have been very difficult for Jesus' disciples to accept the concept of servanthood in leadership because it went against the grain of the Jewish and Graeco-Roman cultural values concerning shame and honor and patronage. The call to humility and the giving up of authority and power as leaders in order to serve others was counter-cultural in Jesus' day (cf. Clarke 2000). Nevertheless, "becoming an effective leader then, much like today, demanded a radical transformation of one's paradigm of leadership and view of authority" (54).

The Biblical Theology of "Servant of the Lord"

Stephen Dempster (2007) provides a very comprehensive study of the terminology, "the servant of the Lord." He traces the meaning from the Old Testament to the New in a chronological and useful fashion. According to Dempster, the concept of the servant of the Lord is a very important biblical theme in the Christian Bible. This concept is found mainly in Isaiah 40–55; John 13, and Philippians 2:6–11. The Hebrew word for servant, *ʿebed*, occurs 806 times in the Old Testament. It means that someone subordinates to a master. In the New Testament, the main word used for servant is *doulos*. It appears 127 times.

"Servant" in the Old Testament

When someone is known as a "servant of the Lord" in the Old Testament, it usually refers to someone with a "special relationship to God in which an individual is a subordinate to the divine Lord" (Dempster, 132). The meaning of "servant" (*ʿebed*) in the Old Testament contains two essential thoughts: obedience and work. The expression *ʿebed yhwh*, "servant of Jehovah," is used in the prophecy of Isaiah. The expression appears twenty times in Isaiah and refers to two things: Israel, as a nation (Isaiah 41:8, "Israel, my servant"), or to a Person, the Messiah. Jesus Christ epitomizes the concept of "servant" in Isaiah in what is known as the "Servant Songs" (42:1–4; 49:1–6; 50:4–9; 52:13—53:12). He is seen as the Messiah of Israel, the righteous servant, the mediator of salvation to Israel and to the gentile world (cf. Dempster, 154–160). Isaiah 53 depicts the servant as one who "was led like a lamb to the slaughter," who took the place of sinners by bearing "the sins of many" (vv. 6, 12), and was buried in "a grave with the wicked" (v. 9). The servant would be empowered by the Spirit (49:1–2; 61:1; Luke 4:21). He would offer hope to others as he listened to the Heavenly Father speak (Isa 42:2–3; 50:4–5). Ultimately the suffering servant would be highly exalted (Isa 52:13; 53:12).

"Servant" in the New Testament

The meaning of "servant" (*doulos*) in the New Testament is frequently used to refer to a master's slave (owner and slave relationship). Doulos is also used to denote the relationship between Christ and the followers of Christ (2 Cor 4:5, "bond slave," or "servant of Christ"). Another common term used to denote servant or service is *diakonos*, which means "to serve" or "to wait at table." Jesus Christ epitomizes this concept best as he took upon himself "the form of a servant" (Phil 2:7); and as the Son of Man, he "did not come to be served, but to serve, and to give his life as a ransom for many" (Matt 20:28; Mark 10:45).

Jesus typifies the servant of Isaiah 42 (Dempster, 166–67). The Lord Jesus Christ exemplified servanthood and taught it to his disciples in the New Testament.

Servanthood finds expression in humility (Matt 23:11–12; John 12:24–26), and in meeting the needs of others (Matt 20:26–27; Mark 9:37). The Gospel of John 13:1–38 is a key passage to understanding the Divine One who has become the supreme servant. The foot washing scene casts Jesus as the humble One who defines the role of his disciples—just as he washes others' feet, they are to do likewise. Jesus who is the Promised Messiah (Isaiah's Servant Songs) is the ultimate servant of all (Dempster, 173–74).

The Old Testament points to a time when the Savior would be born to offer his life as a ransom for many. In the New Testament, Jesus Christ fulfills the prophecies of Isaiah as the servant who offered his life in humility and sacrifice.

Modeling Servant Leadership by Jesus Christ for His Disciples—Matthew 20:20–28

In Matthew 19:28, upon hearing Jesus' promise of a special place for his twelve disciples, James and John coveted the choice places among the disciples. To achieve their ambition, they enlisted their mother to speak on their behalf—requesting to be seated on the right hand and left hand with Jesus in his Kingdom. This angered the other disciples. In response to that request, Jesus gathered them together and began to teach them what it meant to be "great" in his Kingdom.

In the Gospel of Mark, John and James approached Jesus directly (Mark 10:35); however, in Matthew's account, their mother came before Jesus. She could have been Salome (cf. Mark 15:40; Matt 27:56), and this would mean that she was Jesus' aunt, the sister of Jesus' mother, Mary (cf. John 19:25). If this relationship was true, then this manner of approach would seem to add leverage to the request made to Jesus. In his reply, Jesus aimed his attention at the two sons, not the mother (a shift of attention from verse 21 to 22: "You do not know what you are asking"; the second-person plural pronouns are used), (Blomberg 1992, 306; Carson 1984, 430; France 2002, 415; Hagner 1995, 580). Hutchison (2009) provides a succinct and useful argument to help us understand the cultural context of the brothers' and mother's request to Jesus, as it relates to the concept of patronage and kinship ties; and the idea of honor and shame, as it relates to the model of servant-leadership (60–62). These values point to the challenges that Jesus' disciples (then and now) have to face in order to accept and apply Jesus' counter-cultural paradigmatic view of leadership. In a culture which places great value in honor, and avoids shame at all cost, what Jesus had to offer was not readily embraced.

The Zebedee brothers (James and John) and mother (Salome) could have been family to Jesus' mother, Mary. Given this premise, it would be an accepted practice for the Zebedee brothers and their mother to ask for favors from "powerful" family members. "People of power and wealth often served as patrons or benefactors to others, providing access to goods, protection, debt relief, or opportunities for employment or advancement to an office or position in government" (Hutchison, 10). In this case, James and John believed Jesus to be the Messianic King and felt they were entitled to some favors from Jesus (as patron or benefactor), and that their request would be seen as legitimate.

Jesus responded to the brothers directly (as in Mark 10:38) that they did not understand what they were asking. To be associated with Jesus' future glory means first to be associated with his suffering and death. Jesus refers to "suffering and death" as, "Are you able to drink the cup as I am about to drink?" This metaphor, "the cup" (*to poterion touto*), which appears in Matthew 26:39; John 18:11; and in the Old Testament (Ps 11:6; 75:8; Isa 51:17, 22; Jer 25:15–28) connotes suffering and shame, especially that caused by God's wrath.

Not only did the brothers not know what they were asking for, they had no clear idea what Jesus would suffer for them. To ask to reign with Jesus was to ask to suffer with him (cf. Matt 10:37–39; Rom 8:17; 2 Tim 2:12; Rev 3:21). Their immediate response, "We are able," seemed short-lived and betrayed their understanding as seen in the fleeing of Jesus' disciples at the hour of crisis (Matt 26:56-75).

Jesus' word confirms that suffering is inevitable and his word is a prophecy that the disciples will suffer and/or be martyred for their faith and association with him: "My cup you shall drink" (James was martyred in Acts 12:2; John was exiled to the island of Patmos, though not martyred, John 21:20–23; Rev 1:9). Jesus is portrayed as one who is always in submission to his Heavenly Father. In Jesus' retort, we see that God reverses the values of the world: true greatness in the Kingdom is about service, not position (Matt 24–27, cf. 19:27–30; 20:16, 19b). The other ten disciples were understandably "indignant" (*genakthsan*) when they heard the Zebedee brothers' request. This incident became reminiscent of an earlier incident recorded in Mark 9:33–37 and Matthew 18:1 when they were debating about who was the greatest among them. Jesus summoned them together and began to draw a contrast between greatness among the "gentiles" or "pagans" (*ta ethne*) and greatness among heirs and co-heirs of the kingdom. The values of the two brothers and the ten disciples were no different—they reflected what the world stood for: quest for power by "the rulers" (*arxontes*) and "the great men" (*megaloi*) who loved "to lord it over [others]" (*katakureuien*) (Carson 1984, 581).

The world's idea of greatness, honor, and prestige are opposed to that of Kingdom values as espoused by Jesus Christ (Matt 18:1–4). Under the Roman Empire the Jewish people experienced domination and authoritarianism, and sadly these values pervaded the Jewish community (Blomberg 1992, 308). Therefore, in Matthew 20:26 Jesus says, "It is not this way among you." Greatness among the community of Christ is based on service. Anyone who wants to be great must become a "servant" (*diakonos*) of all (cf. Matt 23:11; Mark 9:35). The word "servant" in this context does not refer to a deacon or minister in the church. It is the act, not the position (Blomberg, 307; Carson 1984, 432; France, 417; Hagner 1995, 582; Keener, 309).

The words "great" (*megas*) in verse 26, and "first" (*protos*) corresponds with the request of the Zebedee brothers ("right hand" and "left hand" would be first and second). Jesus repeats the concept of service in verse 27 with a more forceful word, "slave" (*doulos*). The same word is used in 1 Corinthians 9:19; 2 Corinthians 4:5; 1 Peter 5:13. Hence, greatness in the kingdom is a paradoxical idea as opposed to the world's understanding (Matt 10:39; 16:25; 19:30). The disciples are called to follow in the footsteps of their Lord and to follow him in his example of humility, other-centeredness, and self-sacrifice. The "Son of Man" (Matt

16:27; 19:28) has come to serve man (John 13:1–17; Phil 2:7). He is the exemplar of servant leadership and is the model for the disciples to follow. Yes, they will drink the cup he will drink (v. 22), but the special mission of Jesus as the Son of Man is unique, that is, "to give his life a ransom for many" (Matt 20:28). The word "ransom" (*lytron*) has the idea of purchasing the freedom of a slave. In this verse it is used metaphorically to depict Christ's atoning work on the Cross: a setting free from sin and its penalty at the cost of his sacrifice.

There is a recurring pattern in the New Testament where Jesus begins with the notion that his disciples need to die to self, and followed by Jesus' unique atoning death as a model for them to pattern after, or conversely to begin with Jesus' atoning death and then applied to the disciples (John 12:23–25; Phil 2:5–11; 1 Pet 2:18–25) (Carson 1984, 433; France 2002). In Matthew 20:20–28, Jesus modeled servanthood and demonstrated characterization of true greatness by serving others sacrificially with an attitude of humility and other-centeredness, in contrast to his disciples. He modeled servant-leadership to his disciples so that they would in turn be servant-leaders for the Gospel.

CORRELATING CCL AND JESUS CHRIST'S TEACHINGS USING FRENCH AND RAVEN'S (1959) TAXONOMY OF POWER BASES

In chapter 3, I discussed the subject of Contemporary Confucian Leadership—the three components in CCL; its facets and strategies, its weakest link, and its ethical deficiency. How does CCL compare with *moral servant leadership* based on the ethical teachings of Jesus Christ in Matthew 5:3–12, 17–48, and 20:20–28? Correlating these two paradigms of leadership, using French and Raven's (1959) Taxonomy of Power Bases (cf. table 5.1, p. 96; also chapter 4) shows the contrasts in three main areas: ethical orientation, leadership practices, and leader-follower relationship. In terms of ethical orientation, CCL is one of rule-utilitarian ethics and falls short as ethical leadership (cf. discussion in chapter 3), while the biblical paradigm is grounded upon virtue and deontological ethics.

In the practice of power and authority, the CCL leader is status and positional power conscious, and operates from coercion and reward power bases. The leader who abides by Jesus' teachings is inclined toward referent power base, which is premised upon a leader's moral character rather than on formal title or position.

TABLE 5.1. Comparison and Contrast between CCL and Jesus Christ's Ethical Teachings in Matthew 5:3–12, 17–48, and 20:20–28

	Contemporary Confucian Leadership (Westwood et al. 1992, 1997; Farh and Cheng 2000; Lowe 2003; Silin 1976; Redding 1993)	Jesus Christ's ethical teachings Matthew 5:3–12, 17–48; 20:20–28
Ethical system	Rule-utilitarian	Virtue and deontological
Practice of power and authority (labeled by French and Raven 1959)	Status and positional power consciousness: High control, low trust: centralization of decision making, non specificity of expectations, secrecy, protection of dominance, non-emotional ties, and social distance Coercion and reward power bases: Avoidance of formality to avoid accountability, cliques and political manipulation, reputation building and networking. Didactic leadership Aloofness and social distance, centralization of control, ambivalent stance, protection of dominance, patronage and nepotism, reputation building	Referent power base: Spiritual/moral formation-virtue ethics Matthew 5:3–12 (Beatitudes): Poverty of spirit, sin mourners, humility, God-righteousness seekers, pure, merciful, peacemakers, persecution for God-righteousness Matthew 5:17–48 (six ethical case studies): Murder, Adultery, Divorce, Oaths, Retaliation, Enemy-Love Matthew 20:20–28: Servant-principled leadership: Humility, sacrifice, service

Ethical system	Rule-utilitarian	Virtue and deontological
Outcome: leader-follower relationship	Security for followers, disempowerment, dependence, compliance, abuse and misuse of power, patronage and nepotism, cronyism, uncritical, conforming followership (Kelly 1992). Transactional leadership (Kanungo and Mendoca 1996)	Moral forming, Christlike humble servant-leaders who do not abuse power and authority Followers are empowered and independently effective
Summary	Authoritarian, benevolent, and moral leader	Godly, ethical, moral, Christlike humble servant-leader

The use of the different power bases produces respective outcomes in terms of leader-follower relationship. Leaders who use referent power do not abuse or misuse their position or authority; instead they lead by example. Their followers are willing, independent, critical, and ethically sound. Followers are empowered to lead independently and follow interdependently, without fear or reprisal. In this regard, referent power based leadership is most credible and effective. The CCL leader's tendency toward coercion and reward power bases breeds dependent, compliant, and uncritical followership. The follower submits to the leader either reluctantly, under coercion; or willingly, in return for security or rewards. According to Kanungo and Mendoca (1996), CCL resembles transactional leadership and bears its negative features (cf. discussion in chapter 4; also table 4.2, p. 64). Moreover, CCL influences the leader to abuse power, and to practice patronage and nepotism, all of which can lead to corruption (cf. discussion in chapter 6). These are the negative outcomes of the authoritarian-benevolent components of CCL. However, CCL does have its positive aspect. Engaging referent power base in the moral-obligatory component, the CCL leader brings harmony to people—building goodwill between the leader and the follower, and among followers (cf. Table 4.1, p. 56).

The essential posture of Contemporary Confucian Leadership is paternalistic-authoritarian, while that of moral servant leadership is godly, ethical-moral, Christlike servanthood.

INTEGRATION OF ETHICAL TEACHINGS OF JESUS (MATT 5 AND 20)

The Beatitudes (Matt 5:3–12) list the necessary qualities in the moral formation of the Christian disciple or leader. These qualities are humility (v. 3), mournfulness (v. 4), meekness (v. 5), pursuit of righteousness (v. 6), mercy (v. 7), purity in heart (v. 8), peacemaking (v. 9), endurance of suffering for righteousness (vv. 10–12). These are qualities that define the core of one's being which lead to moral conduct and practices. At the fundamental level, this inner character core begins with a trust in God and God's prescription for living a fulfilled and blessed life. This calls for God-dependence, aligning with God's values, fulfilling God's desires, and accepting God's promise of blessing. The Christian disciple or leader eschews self-dependence, worldly values, preoccupation with selfish agendas, and the pursuit of worldly success and happiness. Hence, the Beatitudes constitute the moral foundation for character formation in servant leadership. For the Christian disciple/leader, character formation is a continuous process of yielding to God through the power of the Holy Spirit working in one's life. This is called the process of sanctification.

The six ethical case studies (Matt 5:17–48) illustrate the moral and ethical outworkings of a life that is built upon the Beatitudes. These six cases—murder (vv. 21–26), adultery (vv. 27–30), divorce (vv. 31–32), oaths (vv. 33–37), retaliation (vv. 38–42), and love for enemies (vv. 43–48)—involve relationships between people and were traditionally regulated by laws. However, a greater law, which issues from a transformed heart, is far superior to man-made laws in motivation and outcome. Jesus' reinterpretation of the law in this section underscores the essence of inner righteousness in a person—the purity and the uprightness of one's heart—that goes beyond superficial adherence to rules and regulations.

The Beatitudes and the six ethical case studies reflect an existing tension between biblical values and worldly and/or cultural values. Just as in Jesus' day, disciple-leaders of today are in danger of succumbing to non-biblical values of self-sufficiency, self-righteousness, assertiveness, selfish ambition and desire, vindictiveness, craftiness and deceitfulness, contentiousness, cowardice, extreme anger, covetousness, duplicity, hatred, and vicious ill will.

Contending against these opposing values, Christian disciples are called to live a counter-cultural life. In the realm of leadership, Jesus' model of servanthood (Matt 20:20–28) becomes the normative pattern. As in Matthew 5, Matthew 20 challenges the disciple/leader toward God-dependence, alignment with God's values, and fulfilling God's purposes. Contrary to the world's idea of greatness as "lording over others," Jesus teaches that true greatness lies in serving others. This Christlike humility demands a disposition of vulnerability over self-preservation and self-interest. Moreover, the servant leader seeks to serve God's purposes rather than personal ambitions and desires. In the understanding of servanthood as modeled by Jesus, the servant serves, and is answerable to, his or her Master. The servant recognizes that he or she has been entrusted with resources by the Master to carry out the given tasks. In that regard, servanthood entails stewardship as a trust from God. The Christian disciple/leader exercises that stewardship through the responsible use of delegated power and authority.

The following section highlights three vital aspects of moral servant leadership based on Matthew 5:3–12, 17–48, and 20:20–28: (1) character formation in moral servant leadership; (2) vulnerability in moral servant leadership; (3) stewardship in moral servant leadership.

Character Formation in Moral Servant Leadership

Rinehart (1998) contrasts the difference between those who abuse their power or authority in their leadership and those who lead as servant leaders (cf. table 5.2, p. 100). He makes the observation concerning the temptation a Christian leader might face: "The temptation that each of us faces is to cross out the word *servant* and underline *leader*: Reality, though, does not demand an either/or choice but a continuum that acknowledges the journey we are all traveling. In other words, we are not either a power leader or servant leader, but we are at times one or the other, or somewhere between the two. So many of our leadership motivations, practices, and outcomes originate from who we are before God and where we are in our walk with Him" (160–61).

From table 5.2, we see that servant leaders possess godly characters in terms of their leadership practice. Their character traits contrast starkly with those of power leaders whose focus is upon themselves—they assert themselves to "command and control."

TABLE 5.2. Comparisons Between Power-Leaders and Servant-Leaders (adapted from Rinehart 1998, 161).

Power-leaders	Servant-leaders
Feed on the spotlight	Share the spotlight with others
Make themselves the focal point	Make Jesus the focal point
Seldom develop other leaders	Develop others to become leaders
Have a high turnover as people leave the ministry	Have a low turnover because people stay and are loyal
Keep the focus on themselves and their self-interest and agenda	Make Christ the central focus and agenda
Keep agendas to themselves	Affirm and participate in kingdom agendas
Command and control by keeping power to themselves	Are committed to being a servant first and foremost
Leave people feeling hurt and abused	Are committed to reconciliation and relationships
Refer to their title frequently	May have a title but seldom refer to it
Are masters of manipulation and/or abuse those who get in their way	Respect people for their freedom to think, act, and respond
Use power images, offices, and perks to reveal their place	Abhor the thought of using power images
Pull rank to get their way	Never abuse people or get their way only
Recruit many followers for their work	Develop many followers for the Lord

The idea of servanthood is a question of nature, or character, not one of function, style of leadership, or roles that the leader carries. The servant is *who* he is, not *what* he does. The motivation behind the person who serves as a servant leader is his or her mindset and heart attitude. Marshall (1991) clearly delineates true servanthood from one that is not:

> A person can carry out all the duties or functions of a servant, or do the tasks that a servant has to do, but do it unwillingly or resentfully or just for the money. The person on the receiving end of what is being done soon becomes aware of the lack of real service.
>
> Often a person genuinely and willingly serves but sees service as a means to an end, that end being to rise to a position where you no longer have to serve people but have other people serving you; . . . now it is their turn to sit back and give the orders and watch other people jump to it for a change.
>
> Some undertake all manner of tasks and duties but it is a burden to them. They refuse to delegate . . . yet they grumble . . . [and] end up being so busy doing everything themselves that they have no time or energy to lead and are conscious that in spite of all their hard work they are failing.
>
> Other leaders take on a multiplicity of activities and responsibilities, not because they want to serve but in order to make themselves indispensable, because when they are indispensable they wield real power. (68–69)

The character of leaders is inseparable from the way Christian leadership is exercised (cf. Richards and Hoeldtke 1980, 119–21; Wright 2000, 104–5). Servanthood reveals who they are because Christian leadership involves interaction with the lives of people they work with. Pretending to be pious just so that they can win the hearts of others will only bring them so far. Ultimately, who they are will be revealed when their "dark side" is uncovered.

Os Guinness (1999), in discussing the essential qualities of a worthy leader, asserts that "character is essential and central to good leadership" (11). On character, Guinness highlights three recurring motifs—"core, consistency, costs" (12). Character refers to the core of the person; it requires a consistent display of daily routine where one's true self is open for all to see; the cost of character is "revealed most clearly in the crucible of testing" (13). Guinness answers the question: why does character count in leadership? Externally, it provides the linkage of trust between leader and follower, and internally, character can be likened to "part-gyroscope, part-brake" which are the "leader's strongest source of bearings and restraint, . . . the first prompting to do good and the last barrier against doing wrong are the same—character" (19–20).

Vulnerability in Moral Servant Leadership

Shaw (2006), in his argument for a theological approach to understanding Christian leadership, calls his readers to appreciate the value of theocracy as opposed to democracy or autocracy. He suggests that leaders ought to see themselves as, "first and foremost, servants and followers under the authority and leadership of God, and from that position lead others" (121). Democracy and autocracy are embedded in the fall of man—stemming from fear of autocratic leadership and fear of loss of control. Citing Jesus' ministry, Shaw states that Jesus' lordship (Matt 3:17) is found in his relationship with his Heavenly Father, not "in the extent of his power and influence over his followers" (125).

To cultivate transformational leadership, Christian leaders must have the courage to exercise vulnerable authority—particularly in high-grid (read as high power distance culture) societies where being vulnerable is the last thing any leader would do. "The concern for image in honor-shame societies" (130) is another word for hypocrisy. Shaw acknowledges that in such societies, it is difficult to be vulnerable, and yet when leaders avoid vulnerability, it is as if they have already attained perfection and hence have no need for the cross. "Only when leaders are willing to be vulnerable—with self and with God—can they avoid the pitfalls of the abuses of autocracy and the paralysis of democracy, and truly serve with authority. Only when they are willing and able to hear and receive valid criticism without being controlled by it, only then can they aspire to excellence as individuals and as leaders of God's people" (131).

To act transparently, presupposes that a Christian leader operate from the standpoint of security in Christ's love. The Christian leader rests upon the fact that because she is loved unconditionally and accepted by God, she has a secure sense of self-worth. Christian leaders, who refrain from a performance-based mentality, will be secure in their vulnerability. Willing to admit mistakes and learn from mistakes, they are servant leaders who are not too proud to learn from others and grow toward Christlikeness. They operate not from the standpoint of superiority over others, but from the standpoint of servanthood. They confess their shortcomings to others in order to be authentic and not phony. They recognize their own humanness in terms of weaknesses and shortcomings. They do not portray a façade of infallibility, but they manifest brokenness—a willingness to ask for forgiveness and make restitution to work toward healthy working relationships. Vulnerability lends credibility to the Christian leader who serves interdependently with others.

Stewardship in Moral Servant Leadership

Authority or power is involved in all forms of leadership. The exercise of authority in leadership is a form of stewardship. How a servant leader uses that authority is a question of integrity and a servant's heart. In his inductive Bible study of leaders and leadership in both the Old and New Testaments, Gangel (1997) gives a description of Christian leaders and their use of authority: "Above all, they exercise leadership as servants and stewards, sharing authority with their followers and affirming that leadership is primarily ministry to others, modeling for others and mutual membership with others in Christ's body" (64). Servant leaders exercise their power or authority responsibly without abuse or tyranny. Jesus "did not come to be served, but to serve" (Matt 20:28). He loved those he served (John 13:1–17). In humility, "He emptied Himself" (Phil. 2:7). "Greatness among the community of Christ is based on service. Anyone who wants to be great must become a "servant" (*diakonos*) of all (cf. Matt 23:11 and Mark 9:35).

Shaw (2006) sees the imperative of servant leadership as one that is "built not on power and control but on a proven and trusted record of self-sacrifice, service, and empowerment" (128). Shaw advocates a transformation of leadership that is free from a "controlling follower-developing" type to an "empowering leader-development" type, where Christian leaders are freed from the need to find significance in their roles, but instead, find significance solely through their relationship with God.

Explaining the verses in the Gospel of Mark 9:35b and 10:43b–44, Estep (2005) discusses the idea of stewardship in servant leadership: "The Christian administrator views authority as coming from God. He serves as a steward of that authority and understands that he is to perform the duties of his office with an attitude of humility and service. We are not to use our position to *lord* or *exercise authority over* our partners in ministry. Servanthood leads from relationship, not position. . . . Leading as a servant invites others to join in the ministry as servants" (italics author's, 46).

Servant leadership is stewardship from God. Leaders are entrusted with the responsibility to lead, not as though they are owners of those whom God has entrusted to them, but as stewards. Oftentimes, they forget that theirs is delegated authority, and they wittingly or unwittingly misuse power or authority associated with their roles and responsibilities. They fail to remember that they are God's under-shepherds; they are there to serve those whom God puts under their charge and not to be served by them. Servant leadership calls for responsible stewardship.

SUMMARY

Given the prevalence of the practice of CCL among leaders who are in Christian ministry in Confucian societies, the teachings of Jesus Christ on character virtues (in Matt 5:3–12, 17–48) and on servanthood (in Matt 20:20–28) serve as pivotal values in the face of the challenge of CCL practices, particularly in the misuse of power and authority.

First, I discussed the Sermon on the Mount (SOTM, Matt 5–7) which provides the moral vision for the Christian leader to develop virtues and biblical principles for godly conduct. The ethical teachings of Jesus in Matthew 5:3–12 and the six ethical case studies in Matthew 5:17–48 are congruent with virtue and deontological ethics—they deal with character formation and conduct of the individual with God and with others.

Second, in relation to understanding and exercising of authority and power in Christian ministry, servanthood (Matt 20:20–28) is a key biblical model for the Christian leader. This is a counter-cultural paradigm in Jesus' day and also in the contemporary world as it advocates serving the interest of others over preserving personal position, power, or prestige. This model of humble, self-giving, and exemplary leadership is normative for the Christian leader. It characterizes the life of Jesus Christ—he came "not to be served, but to serve." It is self-giving (power-giving), not self-seeking (power-hungering).

Third, using the terminology in French and Raven's (1959) taxonomy of power bases, I compared and contrasted the practices and strategies of CCL and the teachings of Jesus Christ in Matthew 5:3–12, 17–48, 20:20–28. Leadership principles drawn from Christ's teaching are grounded on virtue and deontological ethics and referent power. The effect is that such leadership raises the level of ethical leadership and moral development in the followers. On the other hand, the practices of CCL, based on rule-utilitarian ethics, using coercion and reward power bases, produce compliant and expedient followers, This is basically a transactional (high control, low trust) approach to leadership (cf. Kanungo and

Mendoca 1996) and breeds uncritical and conforming followers (Kelley 1992) (cf. discussions in chapter 4).

Fourth, the portrait of the servant leader in Matthew 5 and the servanthood model for leadership in Matthew 20 serve as the framework for moral servant leadership. Three vital aspects of moral servant leadership are character formation, vulnerability, and stewardship. In chapter 6, discussion on these three aspects will be expanded as the principles of integrity, humility, and empowerment, respectively.

6

Counter-Cultural Leadership in Confucian Societies: Leading with Integrity, Humility, and Empowerment

INTEGRITY

INTEGRITY IS ONE OF six universal attributes that reflect good leadership, according to House et al. (2004, 727) in their Global Leadership and Organizational Behavior Effectiveness (GLOBE) research project. Sackmann (2005), writing about "Responsible Leadership: A Cross-Cultural Perspective," concurs that "existing research has shown that, in regard to responsible leadership, the leader's integrity in terms of being honest, just, and trustworthy is important since these personal predispositions are assumed to influence choices of actions" (325, cf. also Glynn and Jamerson 2006, "Principled Leadership: A Framework for Action," 151–71).

Integrity "means having the courage and self-discipline to live by your inner truth. Integrity is a function of feeling whole and perfected . . . [and] means putting truth into practice" (Fairholm 1997, 191). There is direct relationship between character and conduct. Character refers to the kind of person he or she is. A person of integrity is "one who makes a habit of acting reflectively, deliberately, and freely, and who *means* what she says and does. The inner reality corresponds to the outward appearance. There is oneness, integrity" (Holmes 1991, 61). In their extensive research on the attributes that make for credible leadership (Kouzes and

Posner 1993), "honesty" ranks the highest: "they want to know that the would-be leader is truthful and ethical" (14).

> All of us put confidence in people we can trust, those whose character, ethics, and abilities are both predictable and of assured high quality. . . . Leaders whose ethics are elastic, who compromise their values for short-term gain, who accept bribes or offer them to others, who do not keep commitments, who play favourites, who unjustly discriminate against others on the spurious grounds of races, ethnicity, gender, etc., and who treat employees in abusive and disrespectful ways, do not act faithfully towards others and will not be trusted.
>
> Conversely, when leaders have integrity they are trusted. . . . Leaders can lead effectively only if their own personal standards are firmly and fully in place. The task of maintaining integrity, among all the seductions, and ambiguities of life, is both difficult and never ending. But the extent to which it is accomplished is the measure of true leadership. (Morrison 2006, 178)

Speaking Truthfully

Integrity and truthfulness are indispensable character-forming traits for one to lead with credibility (cf. Stanwick and Stanwick 2009, 13–31). Without integrity, a leader loses the right to be one, because he or she has lost the ethos to lead.

During the ensuing months after the Beijing Olympics in August 2008, which was touted as the most expensive and most ostentatious display of national pride, China came under heavy criticism. The Beijing Olympics' opening ceremony was a sham when it came to the question of integrity. Ching Cheong, senior writer of *The Straits Times*, in his article, "Olympics' Opening Ceremony: Paying Lip Service to Integrity," (August 16, 2008, A24), wrote:

> The grand opening of the Olympic Games on Aug 8 truly mirrored the China today. The world saw the material wealth of the country. . . . [T]he opening also revealed the regime's spiritual shortcomings.
>
> People around the world were impressed by the four-hour-long grand spectacle, estimated to have cost US$100 million (S$140 million). . . . But with increasing wealth comes also diminishing ethical standards. By faking a "perfect" image, the grand opening suggested a lack of honesty.

> Worst still, it involved faking at the highest level. The decision to replace a talented but not "cute" child singer with a lip-synching "cute" one, was taken by a member of the politburo of the ruling Chinese Communist Party (CCP).
>
> The CCP did not show "respect for fundamental ethical principles" when it decided to fake a "perfect" image. The message it sent out was that whoever had a less "cute" face would be denied a chance even though qualified, and whoever had a "cuter" look had permission to lie. This was wrong and hurt both children seriously and needlessly.
>
> If it [China] tramples on some universally-held values, to which it vowed subscription, it will sustain exactly the kind of China-bashing which it opposes.

Exercising Justice

There are two universal principles that are supported by 6,500 representatives from a wide range of religious faiths which reach an agreement on a global ethic: "First, all people must be treated humanely regardless. . . . Every person or group, no matter how powerful, must respect the dignity of the others. Second, 'what you wished done to yourself, do to others'" (Johnson 2007, 283; cf. 284).

Likewise, Christian leaders are called to stand for justice—to protect the weak and to mete out justice to those who have abused a fellow human being. Elmer (2006) argues that since righteousness and justice are God's character (Deut 32:4–5; Ps 7:9; 2 Tim 4:8; 1 John 2:1), and God has commanded human leaders to do justice (Mic 6:8), Christian leaders need to take after God's character in the way they treat others, for "they reveal the kind of person God is and the kind of relationships he desires with people everywhere" (176). In other words, they exercise moral judgment—"our ability to distinguish right from wrong, and the commitment to do what is right" (Fairholm 1997, 191). In practical terms, "What would a just leader and follower relation look like? How would I treat another fellow human being? How will I exercise power and authority in the way that I serve another person?" (191)

Hitt, Keats, and Yucel (2003) posit that trust is built when leaders exercise "interactional justice" (i.e., equality in interpersonal treatment that members receive from their leader); "procedural justice" (i.e., procedures used to determine the outcomes processed by their leader); and "distributive justice" (i.e., fairness in outcomes received by members from their leader) (19). "Effective leaders build trust within the organization through displays of integrity and fairness. They demonstrate distributive, procedural, and interactional justice" (28).

Operating Transparently

To be fair to contemporary Confucian leaders in Christian ministry, most, if not all, serve out of a sense of duty (as managers and subordinates, cf. Zaleznik, 1977, 1965; cf. discussion below on cronyism) to their respective organizations or institutions. However, one who engages in the CCL practice of didactic leadership unconsciously opens himself or herself up to dishonesty, injustice, and cover-ups of wrongdoings. One example of such lack of transparency is the tainted milk scandal in China (September 2008) that caused several child-deaths, and an undisclosed number of sick children in China. The scandal involved the now bankrupt China dairy giant, Sanlu Group. The company was found guilty of adding melamine, which caused kidney stones and other ailments, into infant formula to falsely raise its protein count. Driven by greed, those who were responsible tried to keep the scandal secret till it could no longer be contained (cf. Ng, January 4, 2009, "Ex-Sanlu Boss Clawed Her Way to the Top *The Sunday Times*, 27; also, Peh, November 14, 2008, *The Straits Times*, A11; Wong, September 19, 2008, *The Straits Times*, A13; also Arjoon, 2009, 155–71).

The CCL leader is skilled in guarding information and keeping almost everything close to his heart—one would always be left wondering what he was thinking. He would be reluctant to tell you what his real thoughts are—for self-protection, and dominance. Standard policies and accountability, especially in the sensitive areas of financial and personnel matters, are either inadequate or absent. Hence, issues would be settled expediently or secretly, so that the lesser is heard or known, the better it is. In this way, ugly truths can be kept hidden; preferential (non-standard) treatment can be meted out; heavy weight donors and patrons can be placated and pleased; and personal mistakes can be denied or go undetected. The unspoken validation for such practices is the maintenance of communal harmony, and concern for personal and institutional reputation. However, beneath such behaviors and practices lie a whole range of possible ills and dysfunctions (especially from Confucian familial values on authority-submission, authenticity, and empowerment cf. Augsburger 1984, 101–30; Balswick and Balswick 2007, 271–83). Examples are the lack of integrity, selfish values, insatiable ambition, enormous ego, amorality, arrogance, avarice and greed, compulsions, co-dependency, corruption, cowardice, cronyism, cunning deception, favoritism, grandiosity, deep-seated insecurity, megalomania, excessive narcissism, nepotism, passive-aggression, and paranoia. In this regard, the ills that infect leaders and organizations in Asian business and corporations can also infect Christian leaders and organizations as well (cf. Kellerman 2004; Lee-Chai and Bargh 2001; Price 2006).

HUMILITY

The second guiding principle for moral servant leadership is humility. "For any position of leadership and responsibility, the greatest temptations are pride and self-exaltation" (Issler 2001, 75). To avoid the pitfalls of pride and self-exaltation, Issler suggests two "wasting time with God" exercises: (1) confession of our sins of pride both in thought and in action to God and to those whom we can trust to uphold us and walk with us when we are in pain; (2) willingness to serve others, and not ourselves: "Humility is the foundational virtue that issues in serving others" (87). Issler gives eight key characteristics of what humility may look like (76).

1. Treating all people with respect and dignity (Rom 12:16).
2. Associating with people who are marginalized in society (Rom 12:16).
3. Having an honest and accurate appraisal of oneself (Rom 12:3, 16).
4. Honoring others by putting their interest above our own (Gal 6:10; Phil 2:3–4).
5. Sharing power and decision-making processes (1 Pet 5:1–4).
6. Willingness to do menial tasks (John 13:1–6).
7. Submitting oneself to all appropriate contexts of authority and honor identified in the Scriptures (1 Pet 2:18–25).
8. Confessing one's sins before God regularly, and to others as well (1 John 1:8–10; Matt 18:15–17).

In their insightful chapter, "Humility in Leadership: Abandoning the Pursuit of Unattainable Perfection," Hoekstra, Bell, and Peterson (2008, 79–95) propose that if ethics is the study of values and customs of a person or group of persons, then "leadership ethics [may be defined] as the study of the values and customs of those who lead or seek to lead," and hence "humility in leadership becomes a primary ethical consideration" (80). Building on the works of Lencioni (2002), and Marcum and Smith (2007), Hoekstra et al. define humility as follows: "Humility is an appropriate self-awareness that avoids thinking too highly of ourselves, blended with a healthy self-respect that avoids thinking too little of ourselves, allowing us to realistically assess our own accomplishments while continuing the pursuit of our own personal development" (83).

The authors propose that what we see on the outside of a person is a reflection of what is inside that person, and hence, the genesis of humility in leadership lies in a person's worldview and core values. In order to develop the virtue of humility, inner reflection is vital and critical for self-awareness. It requires help and discipline from a mentor, or coach, journaling, meditation and prayer, and "drafting a personal mission statement as a permanent reminder of one's worldview" (86).

A Case Study: Protection of Dominance

This section gives an illustration on the protection of dominance. The case involves a Chinese-speaking church in Singapore whose constituent members attempted to protect the dominance of their ethnic language at the expense of a larger and growing constituent of English-speaking members. These attempts included the denial of a separate English-speaking worship service and ordination of an English-speaking pastor. The Chinese ethnic group, which once was the majority, had gradually become the minority.

The church had reached a membership of nearly five hundred, and there were two services. Both services were conducted with translation. At times, the services were long and tedious. The English-speaking members felt very strongly that a restructuring of the worship services would be a great boost toward church health and growth. The older members, including the founding members, who had labored long and hard during the formative decades of the church's life, felt threatened and were not for the idea.

The church extended a call to an experienced retired senior minister from a foreign country. He was in his early seventies and, understanding the situation at the church, he came with the hope to bridge the chasm between the two-generational, two-language, and two-cultural groups, and also to provide guidance to the younger pastor, with the purpose to see him ordained and take on more pastoral responsibilities.

Within the first year of the senior pastor's tenure, he mooted the idea of ordination for the younger minister. What seemed to be a normal course of events led to very ugly church fights at the business meetings, which were dubbed the "Sunday Matinee." This fracas dragged on for many months, and the outcome was that the younger minister was ordained, in the midst of strong protest. The church whittled down significantly in size (more than half of the members left the church during this period, or were planning to leave), the senior pastor resigned when his two-year contract was due for renewal, and the ordained younger pastor left shortly after.

In the meantime, several ministers came and went, and not one stayed sufficiently long enough to bring about healthy church growth. As far as the restructuring of the worship services was concerned, it was not until a decade later that not one, but two English-speaking services were birthed. But the damage had already been done.

At least two things can be observed. First, one cannot deny the strong influence of national or ethnic culture in any organization or church. After all, most of the founding members of this church were Chinese from mainland China and Hong Kong, who migrated to Singapore many years ago. They were heavily influenced by Confucian values of hierarchy and compliance to authority, especially to seniors and those who were in positions of authority, like the founding members. They wanted to maintain the church as an ethnic-speaking church, with other languages only as sub-groups. They also had genuine human and spiritual needs that only a shepherd who could speak and minister in their "heart" language could offer. Second, the "protection of dominance" as one form of authoritarian disposition was clearly exemplified in this case study, demonstrating the lack of humility.

Ascribed authority in Christian ministry is the "cultural default" in Confucian Asia (cf. Wingeier 2004; Solomon 2000; Hinton 1992). The use of positional power in CCL breeds compliant and uncritical followers.

Followers hardly criticize the leader, even when the church or organization is on the brink of atrophy.

As for leaders, few are those who welcome evaluation and critique of their "anointed" leadership (cf. Chan 2002). "Compliance should not be mistaken for biblical submission to leadership. One acknowledges that at times full agreement over decisions cannot be reached and so one learns to accept this reality. Compliance is another matter. When people in authority call for compliance, they are calling for unthinking, undiscerning obedience. Many religious leaders want this, implying that anyone who differs with them is disloyal, either to them or to the church [or organization]. They believe that compliance and submission are one and the same. . . . We must always distinguish between the prompting of the Spirit on the one hand, and the voice of human authorities on the other" (Smith 1999, 104–5).

Hoekstra et al. (2008) articulate five key foundational ideas that embody humility as an ethic of leadership in practice—fallibility, vulnerability, transparency, inadequacy, and interdependence. (1) Fallibility is the willingness to accept imperfection ("I make mistakes" and "I need your patience"), resulting in authenticity. (2) Vulnerability is asking for forgiveness ("I was wrong" and "I need your forgiveness"), resulting in reconciliation. (3) Transparency is admitting ignorance ("I don't know" and "I need your ideas"), resulting in innovation. (4) Inadequacy is acknowledging mortality ("I can't do it all" and "I need your talents"), resulting in work/life balance. (5) Interdependency is moving from self-centeredness to other-centeredness ("I'm not here for me" and "I need your collaboration"), resulting in talent development (87). They conclude that in order for humility to last a lifetime, a leader needs to be teachable, accountable, and willing to receive feedback (92–93).

Biblical counter-cultural leaders invite followers to critique their decisions; they work to listen to feedback; they ask for forgiveness (they say "I am wrong") when they err, and humbly correct themselves; and they build mutual trust-keeping relationships that serve the purposes of God. This act of humility frees the leader from the dangers of hubris (cf. chapter 5; also Kets de Vries 2003, 2006b).

EMPOWERMENT

The third guiding principle for moral servant leadership is empowerment. "Empowerment is power sharing, the delegation of power or authority to subordinates in the organization" (Lim and Daft 2004, 304). There are at least three important reasons why empowerment is essential in leading an organization: (1) It meets the higher needs of individuals in terms of self-efficacy; it gives them purpose for their existence in the organization; (2) It increases the total amount of power in an organization—sharing power leads to a ripple effect of overall power base; and (3) It frees the leader to envision the future and look at the big picture, and it instills shared-responsibility in the followers (305–7). "[E]ffective teamwork is not about democracy and/or consensus. Leaders make decisions for the good of the team, the well-being of its people, and the effectiveness or results of its ministry. But such leadership need not be power focused or governed by the tyranny of consensus. Rather, a leader defines the rules of participation to reflect inclusiveness in the body of Christ, commitment to the work of the kingdom, and effective communication among team members that understands the essence of mutual submission, weakness, and forgiveness" (Lingenfelter 2008, 100).

A servant-leader serves God's people by empowering them to advance the work of God. He or she empowers his or her followers to be the best they can be through their gifts, strengths, skills, training, and passion (cf. Clinton 1997). An essential part of Jesus' mission when he was on earth was to train his disciples and empower them for service to extend the purpose of God. Jesus empowered them to preach the gospel and heal the sick (Matt 10:5–8); and later, in Matthew 28:18–20, he gave his command to them to carry the message of the cross to the entire world.

Smith, Montagno, and Kuzmenko (2004) list six specific leader initiatives in their servant-leader model as follows: valuing people, developing people, building community, displaying authenticity, providing leadership, and sharing leadership (88). There is a place for delegation and empowerment. Leaders must always let go of the need to want to be in control of people, management (which includes planning, organizing, staffing, directing, and controlling, cf. Fincher 2003, 57–94; Block 1993; Browaeys and Price 2008), and leadership.

Cronyism

One example of disempowerment or leadership control can be seen in the way leadership succession is carried out. In Confucian paternalistic-authority culture, the appointment to the top leadership within an organization or institution is typically a private arrangement, much like in Chinese family businesses (cf. chapter 3; also Kets de Vries 1996). The choice candidate is likely to be one who is favored by the incumbent based on some personal relationship or history. The appointment is unlikely to involve any objective selection or screening process.

In their very insightful study of cronyism and governance in Asia, Khatri, Johnson, and Ahmed (2003) examine the Confucian culture, with its accompanying three national dimensions—collectivist, high power distance/paternalistic, and strong uncertainty avoidance. They posit that the Confucian cultural values and traits, with the accompanying three national cultural dimensions, elevate certain socially desirable behaviors such as loyalty and close personal relationships. However, these lead to three important antecedents of cronyism—overemphasis on loyalty, relationships, and formations of in-groups (61).

Khatri et al. define cronyism as "preferential treatment shown to select associates, without regard to their qualifications, with an expectation of reciprocity" (63). The dynamics of cronyism involves "friend-friend" relationships, overriding organizational charts, and "power-seeking" dynamics that move toward one's self-interests, and this form of relationship may or may not necessarily be long term. "Due to the ability of superiors to reward subordinates flexibly and subjectively, subordinates in turn attempt to cultivate personal ties with superiors and conform to their preferences *proactively* in order to improve or secure their positions. Often, the relationship between superiors and subordinates is one in which *active loyalty* is exchanged for reward" (italics author's, 64).

Khatri et al. also distinguish cronyism from the concepts of favoritism, nepotism, and *guanxi*, though all these concepts are closely inter-linked. Favoritism is broader in scope and involves subjectivity and personal biasness. Nepotism is narrower in scope, though it is similar to cronyism for it involves favoritism as well; however, it is solely based on familial ties, as in family businesses. *Guanxi*, translated into English, refers to "relationship" or "connection." Guanxi, when understood in Asian-Confucian, high-power distance/paternalistic culture, implies "reciprocal obligations" or "exchange of favors" between two or more parties involved (i.e., non-familial, social and interpersonal obligations). The difference between *cronyism* and *guanxi* is that in the former, it may be for short-term mutual beneficial purposes, but in the latter, it may be for a long standing reciprocal exchange of mutual benefits (p. 65).

Khatri et al. make eight propositional arguments that are relevant to my discussion on the issue of succession. (1) Due to the Confucian values of reciprocity seen in the practices of *guanxi*, *renqing*, and relational personalism (cf. chapter 3), "the more a culture emphasizes Confucian values, the greater the importance that is placed on personal relationships" (p. 68). (2) Due to the lack of trust in Confucian societies (i.e., feelings of insecurity, selective trust toward people in general leading to in-group mentality, and hence general distrust of out-group), (cf. Redding 1993; also chapter 3), "in societies where lack of trust in others is widespread, there is greater emphasis on developing and maintaining personal relationships" (p. 70). (3) In high power distance societies where power flows downward, paternalistic authority is exercised (cf. chapter 3)—"the preferential treatment shown by superiors to subordinates and the latter's obligation to return the favor is characteristic of cronyism. In this process, loyalty is displayed as a valued obligation to the superiors" (p. 72). (4) Hence, "in high power distance/paternalistic societies, there is strong emphasis on personal loyalty" (p. 73).

From the above four propositional arguments, Khatri et al. put forth the fifth argument showing the relationship between cronyism and in-group members. (5) "An emphasis on in-groups in Chinese culture, whereby relationships and loyalty take precedence over one's ability and competence, is a major source of crony behavior" (p. 74). The selection of in-group members is based on "relationship and loyalty" over "an objective evaluation of a person's ability" (pp. 73–74). In other words, "given a choice between an employee who has close relationship with high loyalty but low competence, and another employee who has high competence but a distant relationship and low loyalty, the former would be favored and recognized as an in-group member" (p. 74). (6) Cronyism takes place "where the in-group phenomenon is widespread" (p. 75). There is a great discrepancy when it comes to resource allocation, treatment, and rewards between in-group and out-group.

This next propositional argument has to do with the cultural element of uncertainty avoidance, which is defined as "the extent to which members of a culture feel threatened by uncertainty or unknown situations" (Hofstede 1991, p. 113). (7) Strong uncertainty avoidance, along with lack of transparency and a weak organizational structure, often leads to an overemphasis on relationships; organizational members often rely on the backdoor diplomacy to achieve their ends "which in turn leads to crony behavior" (Khatri et al., p. 77). Confucian societies are characterized by strong uncertainty avoidance, with an emphasis on relationships, and preference for informality over formality of a structured environment. "Chinese organizations are characterized by a lack of transparency. Management processes are neither clearly defined nor formalized; . . . responsibilities are often left unspecified and ambiguous; . . . disclosure is low; . . . policies, decisions, and plans are not openly shared and communicated to all" (p. 76). In the arena of politics, the lack of transparency often leads to corruption. The lack of formality leads members of an organization to seek close relationships with key figures in the organization in order to secure personal interests.

The last propositional argument discusses loyalty. (8) "In societies where demonstrated loyalty is rewarded, an overemphasis on loyalty leads to crony behavior" (p. 78). Loyalty is a good trait; however, an overuse or overemphasis of loyalty often leads to dysfunctional outcomes, e.g., patronage: "the act of dispensing favors to individuals regardless of their abilities"—"cronies are tied by bonds of obligation in which *patronage downwards* and *loyalty upwards* are exchanged" (p. 78). Cronyism and its implications for leadership succession can be drawn from the study by Khatri et al. and many others who write about Confucian culture; values; family; social psychology; contemporary Confucian paternalistic authority; power and authority; organizational behavior; Asian business management; views and struggles about contemporary Confucian leadership in Christian ministry; and national cultures. Suffice to say, the literature base on this subject is legion (cf. chapter 3).

There is a plethora of writers who write about Asian business management and leadership, organizational behavior, political science, Confucian culture, and leadership and management theories (such as Alon 2003; Backman 2001, 2004; Chen 2004; Cheung and Chan 2005; Cho 1991; Hooker 2003; Koehn and Leung 2004; Kwok 1992; Lim and Daft 2004; Putti, Koontz, and Weihrich 1998; Pye 1985; Sheh 2003; Redding 1993; Silin 1976; Smith and Zhong 1996; Tjosvold, Wong, and

Hui 2004; Tseng 2005; Westwood 1997; Westwood and Chan 1992; Westwood and Chua 1992).

Writers who write from the cultural, psychological, and various disciplines of social science point of views include Bond 1996; Bond and Hwang 1986; Carl, Gupta, and Javinda 2004; Farh and Cheng 2000; Fu et al. 2008; Hofstede 2001; Kets de Vries 1996; Lee-Chai and Bargh 2001; Slote and DeVos 1998; Yan and Hunt 2005.

Writers with a Christian perspective who struggle to make sense of contemporary Confucian leadership in the light of Scriptures in their various contexts, offer their works (published as well as unpublished), such as Chelliah 2001; Hinton 1992; Kang 2007; Lee 2004; Ling 1999; Oh 2003; Wingeier 2004; Wong 1999.

Leadership succession in contemporary Confucian paternalistic authority culture, enacted through the practice of cronyism, depends on (1) the appointee's level of submissive orientation to the incumbent; (2) the incumbent's confidence that the appointee will not totally undo what the incumbent had built up for the organization or institution; (3) the appointee's alignment with traditional cultural norms, and perception of him by the traditional constituents; (4) the perpetuity of a male candidate, in line with a male-dominant patriarchal culture.

According to several authors (e.g., Kellerman 2008, 2004; Kets de Vries 2003, 1997; Johnson 2007; Lipman-Blumen 2005; Price 2006; Whicker 1996), those who exercise positional power and authority based on coercion and reward bases are more inclined to be manipulative and toxic. Toxic behaviors include violating the basic standards of human dignity, playing to the basest fears and needs of followers, stifling constructive criticism, misleading followers through half truths, failing to nurture other leaders, ignoring incompetence, and promoting cronyism and corruption (cf. Pelletier 2009, 117–40).

Leadership succession is a key area where the practice of empowerment or disempowerment greatly determines the effectiveness of the organization. Empowerment in leadership succession involves (1) adopting an objective and transparent selection process versus subjective choice, e.g., selection criteria (cf. Erickson 1997; MacMillan 1992); (2) executing planned and intentional leadership renewal and transition, versus overstaying one's effectiveness, reluctance to share power, and fear of relinquishing control; and (3) ensuring continuity in fulfilling organizational goals and mission, versus perpetuating personal identity in one's successor. (cf. Corace 2001, "Building a Leadership Pipeline," 309–25; Neo and Chen 2007, 145–88, 317–82).

Rothwell (2001) emphasizes the importance for Succession Planning and Management (SP&M), "which is a deliberate and systematic effort by an organization to ensure leadership continuity in key positions, retain and develop intellectual and knowledge capital for the future, and encourage individual advancement" (p. 6). SP&M is very important because (1) "the continued survival of the organization depends on having the right people in the right places at the right time" (cf. Collins 2001); (2) in today's continuing downsizing trend worldwide, the need to identify and develop promising candidates who are both "high performers" and "high potentials" are vital for the future; and (3) when SP&M is not systematically and purposefully carried out, "incumbents tend to identify and groom successors who are remarkably like themselves in appearance, background, and values," establishing an unhealthy "bureaucratic kinship system" that is based on "homosocial production" (which promotes uniformity and gender discrimination) (pp. 7–9).

One glaring problem related to leadership succession in this culture is when the incumbent knowingly or unknowingly overstays his effectiveness. There are several reasons for such a malaise: (1) the effects of aging (physically, mentally, emotionally, socially); (2) the experience of nothingness (the sense of loss); (3) the *talion* principle (the fear of retribution—feeling of paranoia); (4) the edifice complex (will their successors respect the edifice they have built); and (5) the process of retirement (potential losses—status, recognition, income, physical aging, emotional stress) (cf. Kets de Vries 2003, pp. 27–40; also Schein 2004). In the absence of a formal succession mechanism, any hint of a need for leadership change is perceived as rebellion and insubordination to ascribed authority.

Drucker's (1990) four incisive questions on "people decision" for non-profit organizations are instructive: (1) Are we attracting people we are willing to entrust this organization to? (2) Are we developing them so that they are going to be better than we are? (3) Are we holding them, inspiring them, recognizing them? (4) Are we building for tomorrow, or are we settling for the convenient and the easy today? (p. 155).

Lingenfelter discusses the differences between the "responsible-*for*" and "responsible-*to*" leaders. The former have emotional attachment to their role and results and hence would exercise power and control over others. In contrast, the latter exercise detachment of emotions from their role and results by granting their followers the authority, responsibility, and freedom for them to act, yet at the same time holding them accountable for their results (2008, 133).

This act of empowerment will lead to self-directed responsible team members. The fundamental questions to ask about servant leadership are "Do those served grow as persons? Do they, while being served, become healthier, wiser, freer, more autonomous, more likely themselves to become servants?" (Greenleaf, 13–14; cf. also discussions in chapter 4). "The model of spiritual leadership is not command and control. It is confer and network" (Fairholm, 1997, 189; cf. discussions in chapter 5).

The goal is to build followers who are ideal servant-followers (cf. chapter 4; also Kellerman 2008). They are independent (vs. dependent, cf. discussions in chapter 3, 4, and 5); critical thinkers (vs. group-thinkers, cf. Janis 1997); they engage in active decision making, implementing and evaluating processes and products; they "take on new challenges, follow through on projects without much supervision [when leaders allow them], disagree constructively, and think through the implications of their actions [responsibility and accountability]" (Johnson 2007, 189; cf. 188–98).

Integrity (vs. duplicity, injustice, and secrecy), humility (vs. protection of dominance, self-preservation, self-interest), and empowerment (vs. disempowerment, command and control) are premised upon referent and expert power bases (cf. chapter 4). They are moral transforming servant leadership—based on virtue and deontological ethics (cf. chapter 3; chapter 4; chapter 5). They are not based on positional power bases of coercion and reward—rule-utilitarian ethics (cf. chapter 3).

RECOMMENDATION FOR FUTURE RESEARCH

This study is a conceptual, integrative dissertation, focused on philosophical ethics, cultural dimensions of Idealized and Contemporary Confucian leadership, organizational behavior and psychology, social science leadership theories, power-influence theories, Jesus' teachings in the New Testament concerning ethics and servanthood in leadership.

Further to this book, I recommend that empirical and qualitative research be carried out among Christian leaders in Confucian societies, specifically in Singapore (author's residence). The following are some research questions that can be explored.

How is power and authority perceived and practiced in Christian ministry? Are Christian leaders in Singapore more influenced by Confucian values and practices or biblical virtue and deontological ethics, in their leadership practices? Which one, to what degree, and why? Does the language medium of education affect the way Christian leaders think, feel, and lead their ministries, particularly between the English-educated and the Chinese-educated, in relation to the perceptions and practices in Contemporary Confucian Leadership? Why, and how? What are the influence and correlation of moral formation, and servant-leadership to the theory of transformational leadership; why and how do these relate to biblical leadership? Is Contemporary Confucian Leadership more akin to Transactional Leadership Theory or Transformational Leadership Theory and practice? How, and why?

Insights into how Confucian culture (as a whole or aspects of) helps or hinders servant-leader formation for Christians would be helpful. How far or how close are Christian leaders in Singapore gravitating toward Confucian worldviews, values, and practices in Christian ministry will be an interesting study. How power and authority is exercised in Christian ministry is also a fascinating subject of study.

Quantitative and qualitative research evaluating moral and servant-leader formations that impact Christian leaders' worldviews, values, and practices will be very helpful to ascertain the need for holistic training and educating to encourage godly change. A study can be made across a few Confucian societies to discover divergences as well as convergences; such "cross-cultural" findings will be helpful to those from a Confucian culture who serve in another country with Confucian influence.

SUMMARY

This book presents a counter-cultural paradigm in philosophy and practice of power and authority in Christian leadership that is based on a moral foundation (virtue and deontological ethics) according to the teachings of Jesus Christ in regard to character formation (Matt 5:3–12, 17–48), and servant-leadership (Matt 20:20–28) and is supported by social science power-influence theories and moral leadership studies in Confucian culture that promulgates the practice of paternalistic authority (PA).

The moral challenge for Christian leaders is cultivating a counter-cultural paradigm of ethical or moral leadership which is diametrically opposed to the cultural norm of exercising power based on position, coercion, and reward. In this regard, the key focus for Christian leaders is in the person of Jesus Christ. Jesus modeled servanthood and demonstrated characterization of true greatness by serving others sacrificially in an attitude of humility and other-centeredness, in contrast to his disciples. He exemplified servant-leadership to his disciples so that they would in turn be servant-leaders for the Gospel. The portrait of the servant-leader in Matthew 5 and the servanthood model for leadership in Matthew 20 serve as the framework for moral servant leadership. Three vital aspects of moral servant-leadership include character formation, vulnerability, and stewardship (chapter 5).

As an extended discussion on the three vital aspects of moral servant-leadership, this final chapter highlighted three guiding principles—integrity, humility, and empowerment. In regard to character, moral servant-leaders lead with integrity. They strive for consistency in word and deed; they exercise justice; and they are transparent in their management of information, resources, and their leadership. In this regard, the practice of moral leadership is opposed to didactic leadership, corruption, and reputation building.

In regard to vulnerability, moral servant leaders lead with humility. Following Christ's example of humility, they serve in the interest of others. Their practice is opposed to coercive and reward-power strategies to elicit compliance and dependence, and protection of dominance. They model humility in trust-building relationships by acknowledging fallibility, vulnerability, transparency, inadequacy, and interdependence.

In regard to stewardship, moral servant-leaders practice empowerment. They believe in sharing power and decision making, delegation, and developing future leaders for the good of everyone they lead. They are mindful of the ills of disempowerment such as centralizing control and decision making, patronage, nepotism, cronyism, overstaying their effectiveness, underestimating subordinate's competence, and adopting an ambivalent stance.

Several suggestions were made for future research to validate and advance the study of ethical, moral leadership values, worldviews, and practices, in the light of Scriptures, against the background of Confucian Asia. Insights from future research will definitely clarify perspectives for Christian leaders in their quest to honor God through godly leadership.

May God be honored for his work of grace and truth in my life—"He must become greater; I must become less" (John 3:30).

References

Agee, B. R. (2001). Servant leadership as an effective approach to leadership in the church. *Southwestern Journal of Theology, XLIII* (3), 7–19.

Alon, I. (2003). Some final reflections. In I. Alon, Ed., *Chinese culture, organizational behavior, and international business management*, 243–46. Westport, CT: Praeger Publishers.

American Psychological Association. (2001). *Publication manual of the American Psychological Association* (5th ed.). Washington D.C.: APA.

Anthony, M. (2005). Biblical perspectives of Christian management. In M. J. Anthony and J. Estep Jr., (Eds.), *Management essentials for Christian ministries*, 13–34. Nashville, TN: Broadman & Holman Publishers.

Arjoon, S. (2009). Corporate governance, organizational culture and virtue ethics. In O. T. Chen, Ed., *Organizational behavior and dynamics*, 155–71. New York: Nova Science Publishers, Inc..

Augsburger, D. W. (1984). *When enough is enough*. Ventura, CA: Regal Books.

Backman, M. (2001). *Asian eclipse: Exposing the dark side of business in Asia* (Rev. ed.). Singapore: John Wiley & Sons (Asia) Pte. Ltd.

Backman, M. (2004). *The Asian insider: Unconventional wisdom for Asian business*. New York: Palgrave MacMillan.

Balswick, J. O., and Balswick, J. K. (2007). *The family: A Christian perspective on the contemporary home* (3rd ed.). Grand Rapids, MI: Baker Academic.

Banks, R., and Ledbetter, B. M. (2004). *Reviewing leadership: A Christian evaluation of current approaches*. Grand Rapids, MI: Baker Academic.

Bargh, J. A., and Alvarez, J. (2001). The road to hell: Good intentions in the face of nonconscious tendencies to misuse power. In A. Y. Lee-Chai and J. A. Bargh (Eds.), *The use and abuse of power: Multiple perspectives on the causes of corruption*, 41–55. Philadelphia, PA: Psychology Press.

Bass, B. M. (1985). *Leadership and performance beyond expectations*. New York: The Free Press.

Bass, B. M. (1990). *Bass & Stogdill's handbook of leadership: Theory, research, and managerial applications* (3rd ed.). New York: The Free Press.

Bass, B. M., and P. Steidmeier. (2004). Ethics, character, and authentic transformational leadership behavior. In J. B. Ciulla (Ed.), *Ethics, the heart of leadership* (2nd ed.), 175–96. Westport, CN: Praeger.

Beadles II, N. A. (2000, Fall). Steward-Leadership: A Biblical refinement of servant-leadership, *Journal of Biblical Integration in Business*, 25–37.

Bell, D. A. (1997). A communitarian critique of authoritarianism: The case of Singapore. *Political Theory,* 25 (1), 6–32.

Benner, D. G. (2003). *Surrender to love: Discovering the heart of Christian spirituality.* Downers Grove, IL: InterVarsity Press.

Benner, D. G. (2004). *The gift of being yourself: The sacred call to self-discovery.* Downers Grove, IL: InterVarsity Press.

Benner, D. G. (2005). *Desiring God's will: Aligning our hearts with the heart of God.* Downers Grove, IL: InterVarsity Press.

Bennis, W., and Nanus, B. (1985). *Leaders: The strategies for taking charge* (1st ed.). New York: Harper & Row.

Bevans, S. B. (2004). *Models of contextual theology.* Revised and expanded version. Maryknoll, New York: Orbis Books.

Blanchard, K. H. (2005). *Lead like Jesus: Lessons from the greatest leadership role model of all times.* Nashville, TN: Word Pub. Group.

Block, D. I. (2005). The burden of leadership: The Mosaic paradigm of kingship (Deut 17:14–20). *Bibliotheca Sacra, 162* (647), 259–78.

Block, P. (1993). *Stewardship: Choosing service over self-interest.* San Francisco: Berrett-Koehler.

Blomberg, Craig L. (1992). Matthew. In D. S. Dockery (Gen. ed.), *The New American Commentary,* 22, 21–49, 304–8. Nashville, Tennessee: Broadman Press.

Bond, M. H. (1996). Chinese values. In M. H. Bond (Ed.), *The handbook of Chinese psychology,* 208–26. New York: Oxford University Press.

Bond, M. H., and Hwang, K. K. (1986). The social psychology of Chinese people. In M. H. Bond (Ed.), *The psychology of the Chinese people,* 213–66. Hong Kong: Oxford University Press.

Bretzke, J. T. (2004). *A morally complex world: Engaging contemporary moral theology.* Collegeville, MN: Liturgical Press.

Browaeys, M-J. and Price, R. (2008). *Understanding cross-cultural management.* Essex, UK: Pearson Education Limited.

Burns, J. M. (1978). *Leadership.* New York: HarperCollins Publishers, Inc.

Carl, D., Gupta, V., and Javinda, M. (2004). Power distance. In R. J. House, P. J. Hanges, M. Javinda, P. W. Dorfman, and V. Gupta (Eds.), *Culture, leadership, and organizations: The GLOBE study of 62 societies,* 513–63. Thousand Oaks, CA: Sage Publications.

Carson, D. A. (1978). *The Sermon on the Mount: An evangelical exposition of Matthew 5–7.* Grand Rapids, MI: Baker Books.

Carson, D. A. (1984). Matthew. In F. E. Gaebelien (Gen. ed.), *The Expositor's Bible Commentary,* 8, 3–57, 430–34. Grand Rapids, MI: Zondervan.

Carter, P. (1997). *The servant-ethic in the New Testament.* New York: Peter Lang Publishing, Inc.

Cha, B. K. (1993). *A Confucian theory of leadership: Building Western leadership practice on Eastern thought* (2nd ed.). Seoul, Korea: Parkmungak Publishing Co.

Cha, P., Kang, S., and Lee, H. (2006). *Growing healthy churches.* Downers Grove, IL: IVP.

Chaleff, I. (2003). *The courageous follower: Standing up to and for our leaders.* San Francisco: Berrett-Koehler.

Chan, M. L. Y. (2002). Issues in spirituality, authority and stewardship. *Trinity Theological Journal,* 5 (1), 3–22.

Chan, W. T. (1963). *A sourcebook in Chinese philosophy.* (Wing-Tsit Chan, Trans. and Compiled). Princeton, NJ: Princeton University Press.

Chan, W. T. (1967). The story of Chinese philosophy. In C. A. Moore (Ed.), *The Chinese mind: Essentials of Chinese philosophy and culture,* 31–76. Honolulu: The University Press of Hawaii.

Chang, L. S. (1999). *Asia's religions: Christianity's momentous encounter with paganism.* Phillipsburg, NJ: P&R Publishing.

Charles, J. D. (2004). Do not suppose that I have come: The ethics of the Sermon on the Mount reconsidered. *Southwestern Journal of Theology, 46* (3), 47–70.

Chelliah, E. P. (2001). Values of ministerial effectiveness for pastoral leadership in the TRAC Methodist Churches of Singapore. Unpublished doctoral dissertation, Fuller Theological Seminary, Pasadena, CA.

Chen, C. S. (1991). Confucian style of management in Taiwan. In J. M. Putti (Ed.), *Management: Asian context,* 177–97. Singapore: McGraw-Hill Book Co.

Chen, M. (2004). *Asian management systems: Chinese, Japanese and Korean styles of business.* Bedford Row, London: Thomson Learning.

Cheng, B. S., Chou, L. F., Wu, T.Y., Huang, M. P., and Farh J. L. (2004). Paternalistic leadership and subordinate responses: Establishing a leadership model in Chinese organizations. *Asian Journal of Social Psychology, 7,* 89–117.

Cheong, C. (2008, August 16). Olympics opening ceremony: Paying lip service to integrity. *The Straits Times,* A24.

Cheung, C. K. and Chan, C. F. (2005). Philosophical foundations of eminent Hong Kong Chinese CEOs' leadership. *Journal of Business Ethics, 60* (1), 47–62.

Chikudate, N. (2004). The double-edged sword of organizational culture in Asia. In K. Leung and S. White (Eds.), *Handbook of Asian management,* 245–63. Norwell, MA: Kluwer Academic Publishers.

Ching, J. (1977). *Confucianism and Christianity: A comparative study.* Tokyo, Japan: Kodansha International.

Cho, Dong-Sung (1991). Managing by patriarchal authority in Korea. In J. M. Putti (Ed.), *Management: Asian context,* 15–35. Singapore: McGraw-Hill Book Co.

Ciulla, J. B. (Ed.). (1998). *Ethics, the heart of leadership.* Westport, CT: Praeger Publishers.

Ciulla, J. B. (2003). *The ethics of leadership.* United Kingdom: Thomson.

Ciulla, J. B. (Ed.). (2004). *Ethics, the heart of leadership* (2nd ed.). Westport, CT: Praeger Publishers.

Ciulla, J. B. (2006). Ethics: the heart of leadership. In T. Maak and N. M. Pless (Eds.), *Responsible leadership,* 17–32. New York: Routledge.

Clarke, A. D. (2000). *Serve the community of the church: Christians as leaders and ministers.* Grand Rapids, MI: William. B. Eerdmans Publishing Co.

Clegg, S., Dunphy, D. C., and Redding, S. G. (Eds.). (1986). *The enterprise and management in East Asia.* Hong Kong: Centre of Asian Studies, University of Hong Kong.

Clinton, J. R. (1997). *Mentoring: Developing leaders through empowering relationships: How pastors can train leaders without adding more programs.* Altadena, CA: Barnabas Publishers.

Cloud, H., and Townsend, J. (1995). *Safe people: How to find relationships that are good for you and avoid those that aren't.* Grand Rapids, MI: Zondervan.

Cloud, H., and Townsend, J. (2001). *How people grow: What the Bible reveals about personal growth.* Grand Rapids, MI: Zondervan.

Coe, J. (2000). Musings on the dark night of the soul: Insights from St. John of the cross on a developmental spirituality. *Journal of Psychology and Theology, 28* (4), 293–307.

Coe, J. (2004). *The hidden heart: Why we still sin when we know so much.* Unpublished manuscript, Biola University.

Coe, J. (2005) *The seven deadly disconnects of seminary training: Theological and spiritual formation reflections on a transformational model.* Unpublished manuscript, Biola University.

Collins, J. (2001). *Good to great: Why some companies make the leap . . . while others don't.* New York: HarperCollins Publishers Inc.

Conger, J. A. (1997). The dark side of leadership. In R. P. Vecchio (Ed.), *Leadership: Understanding the dynamics of power and influence in organizations,* 215–32. Notre Dame, IN: University of Notre Dame Press.

Conger, J. A. (1999). *Building leaders: How successful companies develop the next generation.* San Francisco: Jossey-Bass.

Conger, J. A., and Kanungo, R.N. (1998). *Charismatic leadership in organizations.* Thousand Oaks, CA: Sage Publications, Ltd.

Corace, C. (2001). Building a leadership pipeline. In W. H. Mobley and M. W. McCall, Jr. (Eds.), *Advances in global leadership,* 2, 309–25. Kidlington, Oxford, UK: Elsevier Science Ltd.

Creel, H. G. (1953). *Chinese thoughts from Confucius to Mao Tse-tung.* Chicago: The University of Chicago Press.

De Bary, E. O. (2003). *Theological reflection: The creation of spiritual power in the information age.* Collegeville, MN: Liturgical Press.

De Bary, Wm. T. (Ed.). (1960). *Sources of Chinese tradition.* New York: Columbia University Press.

De Bary, Wm. T. (1989a). *The noble man in the Analects.* Singapore: The Institute of East Asian Philosophies, National University of Singapore.

De Bary, Wm. T. (1989b). *Confucius as a noble man.* Singapore: The Institute of East Asian Philosophies, National University of Singapore.

De Bary, Wm. T. (1991). *The trouble with Confucianism.* Cambridge, MA: Harvard University Press.

De Pree, M. (1989). *Leadership jazz.* New York: Doubleday.

De Pree, M. (1997). *Leading without power: Finding hope in serving community.* San Francisco: Jossey-Bass.

De Silva, D. A. (2000). *Honor, patronage, kinship & purity: Unlocking New Testament culture.* Downers Grove, IL: IVP Academic.

Dempster, S. G. (2007). The servant of the Lord. In S. J. Hafemann and P. R. House (Eds.), *Central themes in biblical theology: Mapping unity in diversity.* Grand Rapids, MI: Baker Academics.

Dorfman, P. W., and Howell, J. P. (1997). Leadership in Western and Asian countries: Commonalities and differences in effective leadership processes across cultures. *Leadership Quarterly, 8* (3), 233–75.

Doriani, D. M. (2006). *The Sermon on the Mount: The character of a disciple.* Phillipsburg, NJ: P&R Publishing.

Drucker, P. F. (1990). *Managing the non-profit organization: Principles and practices.* New York: Harper Business.

Elmer, D. H. (2006). *Cross-cultural servanthood: Serving the world in Christlike humility.* Downers Grove, IL: IVP Books.

Engstrom, T. W. (1976). *The making of a Christian leader.* Grand Rapids, MI: Zondervan Publishing House.

Erickson, W. (1997). Transition in leadership. In G. Barna (Ed.), *Leaders on leadership: Wisdom, advice and encouragement on the art of leading God's people*, 297–316. Ventura, CA: Regal Books.

Estep, J., Jr. (2005). A theology of administration. In M. J. Anthony and J. Estep Jr., (Eds.). *Management essentials for Christian ministries*,13–34. Nashville, TN: Broadman & Holman Publishers.

Fairholm, G. W. (1997). *Capturing the heart of leadership: Spirituality and community in the new American workplace*. Westport, CT: Prager.

Farh, J. L., and Cheng, B. S. (2000). A cultural analysis of paternalistic leadership in Chinese organizations. In J. T. Li, A. S. Tsui, and E. Weldon (Eds.), *Management and organizations in the Chinese context*,84–127. New York: St. Martin's Press, Inc.

Farh, J. L., Liang, J., Chou, L. F., and Cheng, B. S. (2008). Paternalistic leadership in Chinese organizations: Research progress and future research directions. In C. C. Chen and Y. T. Lee (Eds.), *Leadership and management in China: Philosophies, theories, and practices*, 171–205. Cambridge: Cambridge University Press.

Fernandez, J. A. (2004). The gentleman's code of Confucius: Leadership by values. *Organizational dynamics*, 33 (1), 21–31.

Fiedler, F. E. (1967). *A theory of leadership effectiveness*. New York: McGraw-Hill.

Fincher, C. (2003). *Administrative leadership in academic governance and management*. Lanham, MD: University Press of America, Inc.

Ford, L. (1991). *The transforming leader*. London: Hodder & Stoughton.

France, R. T. (2002). The Gospel of Mark. In I. H. Marshall and D. A. Hagner (Eds.), *The New International Greek Testament commentary*, 409–21. Grand Rapids, MI: William B. Eerdmans Publishing Co.

Frankena, W. K. (1965). *Three historical philosophies of education*. Glenview, IL: Scott, Foresman and Company.

Frankena, W. K. (2002). A critique of virtue-based ethics (1973). In L. P. Pojman, *Ethical theory: Classical and contemporary readings*, 350–55. Belmont, CA: Wadsworth.

French, Jr., R. P., and Raven, B. (1959). The bases of social power. In M.T. Matteson and J. M. Ivancevich (Eds.), *Management and organizational behavior classics*, 303–19. Boston, MA: Richard D. Irwin, Inc.

Fu, P. P., Wu, R., Ye, J., and Yang, Y. (2008). Chinese culture and leadership. In J. S. Chhokar, F. C. Brodbeck, and R. J. House (Eds.), *Culture and leadership across the world: The GLOBE book of in-depth studies of 25 societies*, 877–907. Mahwah, NJ: Lawrence Erlbaum Associates, Publishers.

Fung, Y. L. (1952). *A history of Chinese philosophy, 1* (2nd ed.). (Derk Bodde, Trans.) Princeton, NJ: Princeton University Press.

Gabrenya Jr., W. K., and Hwang, K. K. (1996). Chinese social interaction: Harmony and hierarchy on the good earth. In M. H. Bond (Ed.), *Handbook of Chinese psychology*, 309–21. Quarry Bay, Hong Kong: Oxford University Press (China) Ltd.

Gangel, K. O. (1997). *Team leadership in Christian ministry: Using multiple gifts to build a unified vision*. (Rev. ed.). Chicago: Moody Press.

Gangel, K. O. (2008). *Surviving toxic leaders: How to work for flawed people in churches, schools, and Christian organizations*. Eugene, OR: Wipf & Stock.

Glynn, M., and Jamerson, H. (2006). Principled leadership: A framework for action. In E. D. Hess and K. S. Cameron (Eds.), *Leading with values: Positivity, virtue, and high performance*, 151–71. New York: Cambridge University Press.

Greenleaf, R. K. (1977). *Servant leadership: A journey into the nature of legitimate power and greatness.* New York: Paulist Press.

Greenman, J. F. (2007). John R. W. Stott. In J. P. Greenman, T. Larsen, and S. R. Spencer, (Eds.), *The Sermon on the Mount through the centuries,* 245–80. Grand Rapids, MI: Brazos Press.

Guinness, O. (Ed.). (1999). *Character counts: Leadership qualities in Washington, Wilberforce, Lincoln, and Solzhenitsyn.* Grand Rapids, MI: Baker Books.

Gula, R. M. (1996). *Ethics in pastoral ministry.* Mahwah, NJ: Paulist Press.

Gustafson, J. M. (1988). *Varieties of moral discourse: Prophetic, narrative, ethical, and policy.* Grand Rapids, MI: Calvin College and Seminary.

Hagberg, J. O., and Guelich, R. A. (2005). *The critical journey: Stages in the life of faith* (2nd ed.). Salem, WI: Sheffield Pub. Co.

Hagner, D. A. (1995). Matthew 14–28. In B. M. Metzger (Gen. ed.), *Word Biblical Commentary, 33B,* 573–83. Nashville, TN: Thomas Nelson Publishers.

Hagner, D. A. (2007). Holiness and ecclesiology: The church in Matthew. In K. E. Brower and A. Johnson (Eds.), *Holiness and ecclesiology in the New Testament,* 40–56. Grand Rapids, MI: William B. Eerdmans Publishing Company.

Hands, D. R., and Fehr, W. L. (1993). *Spiritual wholeness for clergy: A new psychology of intimacy with God, self, and others.* Bethesda, MD: The Alban Institute, Inc.

Hesse, H. (1956). *The journey to the east.* (Hilda Rosner, Trans.) NewYork: Strauss & Giroux.

Hiebert, P. G. (1994). *Anthropological reflections on missiological issues.* Grand Rapids, MI: Baker Books.

Hiebert, P. G. (1995). *Incarnational ministry: Planting churches in band, tribal, peasant, and urban societies.* Grand Rapids, MI: Baker Books.

Hinton, K. W. (1992). *Growing churches Singapore style: Ministry in an urban context.* Cluny Road, Singapore: Overseas Missionary Fellowship (IHQ) Ltd.

Hitt, M. A., Keats, B. W., and Yucel, E. (2003). Strategic leadership in global business organizations: Building trust and social capital. In W. H. Mobley and P. W. Dorfman (Eds.), *Advances in global leadership,* 3, 9–35. Kidlington, Oxford, UK: Elsevier Science Ltd.

Hitt, W. D. (1990). *Ethics and leadership: Putting theory into practice.* Columbus, OH: Brattelle Press.

Hoekstra, E., Bell, A., and Peterson, S. R. (2008). Humility in leadership: Abandoning the pursuit of unattainable perfection. In S. A. Quatro and R. R. Sims (Eds.), *Executive ethics: Ethical dilemmas and challenges for the c-suite,* 79–95. Charlotte, NC: Information Age Publishing, Inc.

Hofstede, G. H. (1980). *Culture's consequences: International differences in work-related values.* London: Sage Publications, Ltd.

Hofstede, G. H. (1991). *Cultures and organizations: Software of the mind.* London: McGraw-Hill Publications.

Hofstede, G. H. (2001). *Culture's consequences: Comparing values, behaviors, institutions, and organizations across nations* (2nd ed.). Thousand Oaks, CA: Sage Publications, Ltd.

Hofstede, G. H. and Hofstede, G. J. (2005). *Cultures and organizations: Software of the mind.* New York: McGraw-Hill Publications.

Hollinger, D. P. (2002). *Choosing the good: Christian ethics in a complex world.* Grand Rapids, MI: Baker Academic.

Holmes, A. F. (1977). *All truth is God's truth*. Grand Rapids, MI: William B. Eerdmans Publishing Company.

Holmes, A. F. (1984). *Ethics: Approaching moral decisions*. Downers Grove, IL: InterVarsity Press.

Holmes, A. F. (1991). *Shaping character: Moral education in the Christian college*. Grand Rapids, MI: William B. Eerdmans Publishing Company.

Hooker, J. (2003). *Working across cultures*. Stanford, CA: Stanford University Press.

House, R. J., Hanges, P. J., Javinda, M., Dorfman, P. W., and Gupta, V. (Eds.). (2004). *Culture, leadership, and organizations: The GLOBE study of 62 societies*. Thousand Oaks, CA: Sage Publications, Ltd.

Hoyk, R., and Hersey, P. (2008). *The ethical executive: becoming aware of the root causes of unethical behavior: 45 psychological traps that everyone of us falls prey to*. Stanford, CA: Stanford University Press.

Hsieh, Y. W. (1967). Filial piety and Chinese society. In C. A. Moore (Ed.), *The Chinese mind: Essentials of Chinese philosophy and culture*, 167–87. Honolulu: The University Press of Hawaii.

Hsu, Francis L. K. (1971). Kinship, society, and culture. In Francis L. K., Hsu (Ed.), *Kinship and culture*, 479–91. Chicago, IL: Aldine Publishing Company.

Hsu, L. K. (1998). Confucianism in comparative context. In W. H. Slote and G. A. De Vos (Eds.), *Confucianism and the family*, 53–71. New York: State University of New York Press.

Hsu, Leonard S. L. (1932). *The political philosophy of Confucianism: An interpretation of the social and political ideas of Confucius, his forerunners, and his early disciples*. New York: E. P. Dutton & Co.

Hughes, R. L., Ginnett, R. C., and Curphy, G. J. (1999). *Leadership: Enhancing the lessons of experience*. New York: Irwin/McGraw-Hill.

Hunter, J. C. (2004). *The world's most powerful principle*. New York: Crown Business.

Hutchison, J. C. (2009). Servanthood: Jesus' counter-cultural call to Christian leaders. *Bibliotheca Sacra, 166* (661), 53–69.

Hybels, B. (2002). *Courageous leadership*. Grand Rapids, MI: Zondervan.

Issler, K. (2001). *Wasting time with God: A Christian spirituality of friendship with God*. Downers Grove, IL: InterVarsity Press.

Janis, I. L. (1997). Groupthink. In R. P. Vecchio (Ed.), *Leadership: Understanding the dynamics of power and influence in organizations*, 161–76. Notre Dame, IN: University of Notre Dame Press.

Ji, Li, Ngin, P. M., and Teo, A. C. Y. (2008). Culture and leadership in Singapore: Combination of the East and the West. In J. S. Chhokar, F. C. Brodbeck, and R. J. House (Eds.), *Culture and leadership across the world: The GLOBE book of in-depth studies of 25 societies*, 947–68. Mahwah, NJ: Lawrence Erlbaum Associates, Publishers.

Johnson, C. E. (2005). *Meeting the ethical challenges of leadership: Casting light or shadow* (2nd ed.). Thousand Oaks, CA: Sage Publications, Inc.

Johnson, C. E. (2007). *Ethics in the workplace: Tools and tactics for organizational transformation*. Thousand Oaks, CA: Sage Publications, Inc.

Kang, C. (2007, March 3). Asian American churches face leadership gap. *Los Angeles Times*, B2.

Kanungo, R. N., and Mendoca, M. (1996). *Ethical dimensions of leadership*. Thousand Oaks, CA: Sage Publications, Inc.

Kao, H., and Young, L. (1992). The individual and the organization. In R. I. Westwood (Ed.), *Organisational behaviour: Southeast Asian perspectives*, 265–84. Quarry Bay, Hong Kong: Longman Group (Far East) Ltd.

Keener, Craig S. (1997). Matthew, In Grant Osborne (Series ed.), *The IVP New Testament Commentary Series*, 294–311. Downers Grove, IL: InterVarsity Press.

Kellerman, B. (2004). *Bad leadership: What it is, how it happens, why it matters*. Boston, MA: Harvard Business School Press.

Kellerman, B. (2008). *Followership: How followers are creating change and changing leaders*. Boston, MA: Harvard Business Press.

Kelley, R. E. (1992). *The power of followership: How to create leaders people want to follow and followers who lead themselves*. New York: Doubleday.

Kelman, H. C., and Hamilton, V. L. (1989). *Crimes of obedience: Toward a social psychology of authority and responsibility*. New Haven and London: Yale University Press.

Kets de Vries, M. F. R. (1996). *Family business: Human dilemmas in the family firm*. London: International Thomas Business Press.

Kets de Vries, M. F. R. (1997). Leaders who self-destruct: The causes and cures. In R. P. Vecchio (Ed.), *Leadership: Understanding the dynamics of power and influence in organizations*, 233–45. Notre Dame, IN: University of Notre Dame Press.

Kets de Vries, M. F. R. (2003). *Leaders, fools and imposters: Essays on the psychology of leadership* (Rev. ed.). Lincoln, NE: iUniverse, Inc.

Kets de Vries, M. F. R. (2006a). *The leader on the couch: A clinical approach to changing people and organizations*. West Sussex, UK: John Wiley & Sons Ltd.

Kets de Vries, M. F. R. (2006b). *The leadership mystique: Leading behavior in the human enterprise*. Harlow, UK: Prentice Hall.

Kets de Vries, M. F. R., and Miller, D. (1997). Narcissism and leadership: An object relations perspective. In R. P. Vecchio (Ed.), *Leadership: Understanding the dynamics of power and influence in organizations*, 195–214. Notre Dame, IN: University of Notre Dame Press.

Khatri, N., J. P. Johnson, and Z. U. Ahmed. (2003). A two-stage model of cronyism in organizations: A cultural view of governance. In J. B. Kidd and F-J. Richter, Eds., *Corruption and governance in Asia*, 61–85. New York: Palgrave MacMillan.

Koehn, D., and Leung, A. S. M. (2004). Western and Asian business ethics: Possibilities and problems. In K. Leung and S. White (Eds.), *Handbook of Asian management*, 265–81. Norwell, MA: Kluwer Academic Publishers.

Kouzes, J. M, and Posner, B. Z. (1993). *Credibility: How leaders gain and lose it, and why people demand it*. San Francisco: Jossey-Bass Publishers.

Kraft, C.H. (1989). *Christianity with power: Your worldview and your experience of the supernatural*. Eugene, OR: Wipf & Stock Publishers.

Kung, H., and Ching, J. (1989). *Christianity and Chinese religions*. New York: Doubleday and Collins Publishers.

Kwok, L. (1992). Groups and social relationships. In R. I. Westwood (Ed.), *Organisational behaviour: Southeast Asian perspectives*, 243–64. Quarry Bay, Hong Kong: Longman Group (Far East) Ltd.

Lam, Y. L. J. (2002). Defining the effects of transformational leadership on organizational learning: A cross-cultural comparison. *School Leadership and Management*, *22*(4), 439–52.

Lee, E. S. (2004). Transformational leadership among selected senior pastors in Korea. Unpublished doctoral dissertation, Trinity International University, Deerfield, IL.

Lee, H. S. (2001). Paternalistic human resource practices: Their emergence and characteristics. *Journal of Economic Issues, XXXV* (4), 841–69.

Lee-Chai, A. Y., and Bargh, J. A. (Eds.). (2001). *The use and abuse of power: Multiple perspectives on the causes of corruption*. Philadelphia: Psychological Press.

Legge, J. (1930). *The four books: Confucian Analects, the great learning, the doctrine of the mean, and the works of Mencius* (English Translation). Shanghai: The Chinese Book Company.

Legge, J. (1960). *The Chinese classics: The Shoo King or the book of historical documents*. Vol. III. Hong Kong: Hong Kong University Press.

Leung, K. (1996). The role of beliefs in Chinese culture. In M. H. Bond (Ed.), *Handbook of Chinese psychology*, 247–62. Quarry Bay, Hong Kong: Oxford University Press (China) Ltd.

Lim, G. S. and Daft, R. L. (2004). *The leadership experience in Asia*. Singapore: Thomson Learning.

Ling, S. (1999). *The "Chinese" way of doing things: Perspectives on American-Born Chinese and the Chinese church in North America*. Phillipsburg, NJ: P&R Publishing.

Lingenfelter, S. G. (2008). *Leading cross-culturally: Covenant relationships for effective Christian leadership*. Grand Rapids, MI: Baker Academic.

Lipman-Blumen, J. (2005). *The allure of toxic leaders: Why we follow destructive bosses and corrupt politicians—and how we can survive them*. New York: Oxford University Press.

Low, K. C. (2006). Father leadership: the Singapore case study. *Management Decision, 44* (1), 89–104.

Lowe, S. (2003). Chinese culture and business management. In I. Alon (Ed.), *Chinese culture, organizational behavior, and international business management*, 1–25. Westport, CT: Praeger Publishers.

Maak, T., and Pless, N. M. (2006). Responsible leadership: a relational approach. In T. Maak and N. M. Pless (Eds.), *Responsible leadership*, 33–53. New York: Routledge.

MacArthur, J. F. (1985). Matthew 1–7. *The MacArthur New Testament commentary*. Chicago: Moody Press.

MacInytre, A. (1981). *After virtue*. Notre Dame, IN: University of Notre Dame Press.

MacMillan, P. (1992). *Hiring excellence: Six steps to making good people decisions*. Colorado Springs, CO: NavPress.

Malphurs, A. (2003). *Being leaders: The nature of authentic Christian leadership*. Grand Rapids, MI: Baker Books.

Marshall, T. (1991). *Understanding leadership: Fresh perspectives on the essentials of New Testament leadership*. Chichester, UK: Sovereign World Ltd.

McEwan, T. (2001). *Managing values and beliefs in organisations*. Essex, UK: Pearson Education Limited.

McIntosh, G. L., and Rima, Sr., S. D. (1997). *Overcoming the dark side of leadership: The paradox of personal dysfunction*. Grand Rapids, MI: Baker Books.

Means, J. E. (1989). *Leadership in Christian ministry*. Grand Rapids, MI: Baker Books.

Mei, Y. P. (1960). Confucius: Selections from the Analects. In W. T. De Bary, W. T. Chan, and B. Watson (Compilers), *Sources of Chinese tradition*, 17–35. New York: Columbia University Press.

Mei, Y. P. (1967). The basis of social, ethical, and spiritual values in Chinese philosophy. In C. A. Moore (Ed.), *The Chinese mind: Essentials of Chinese philosophy and culture*, 149–66. Honolulu: The University Press of Hawaii.

Miller, C. (1995). *The empowered leader: 10 keys to servant leadership*. Nashville, TN: Broadman & Holman Publishers.

Moore, C. A. (1967). Introduction: The humanistic Chinese mind. In C. A. Moore (Ed.), *The Chinese mind: Essentials of Chinese philosophy and culture*, 1–10. Honolulu: The University Press of Hawaii.

Morrison, A. (2006). Ethical standards and global leadership. In W. H. Mobley and E. Weldon (Eds.), *Advances in global leadership*, *4*, 165–79. Kidlington, Oxford, UK: Elsevier Science Ltd.

Neo, B.S., and Chen, G. (2007). *Dynamic governance: Embedding culture, capabilities and change in Singapore*. Singapore: World Scientific Co., Pte. Ltd.

Ng, G. (2009, January 4). Ex-Sanlu boss clawed her way to the top: Tian Wenhua insists she isn't the only one to blame for melamine tragedy. *The Sunday Times*, 27.

Northouse, P. G. (2004). *Leadership: Theory and practice* (3rd ed.). Thousand Oaks, CA: Sage Publications, Inc.

Nouwen, H. J. M. (1991). *In the name of Jesus: Reflections on Christian leadership*. New York: Crossroad.

Oh, M. S. (2003). Study on appropriate leadership pattern for the Korean church in postmodern era. *Journal of Asian Mission*, 5 (1), 131–45.

Olekalns, M. (2004). In the eye of the beholder: Culture and the perception of organizational justice. In K. Leung and S. White (Eds.), *Handbook of Asian management*, 415–38. Norwell, MA: Kluwer Academic Publishers.

Pazmino, R. W. (1994). *By what authority do we teach?: Sources for empowering Christian educators*. Grand Rapids, MI: Baker Books.

Peh, S. H. (2008, November 14). Being fake is very real in China: But cutting corners to make cheaper products is now costing lives. *The Straits Times*, A11.

Pelletier, K. L. (2009). Toxic leadership as an antecedent to organizational corruption. In O. T. Chen (Ed.), *Organizational behavior and dynamics*, 117–40. New York: Nova Science Publishers, Inc.

Peterson, M. L. (2001). *With all your mind: A Christian philosophy of education*. Notre Dame, IN: University of Notre Dame Press.

Pojman, L. P. (2000). *The moral life: An introductory reader in ethics and literature*. NY: Oxford University Press.

Pojman, L. P. (2002a). *Ethics: Discovering right and wrong* (4th ed.). Belmont, CA: Wadsworth/Thomson Learning.

Pojman, L. P. (2002b). *Ethical theory: Classical and contemporary readings. Belmont, CA: Wadsworth.*

Porter, B. E. (2000, Fall). A response to stewardship-leadership: A biblical refinement of servant-leadership. *Journal of Biblical Integration in Business*, 38–42.

Pratto, F., and Walker A. (2001). Dominance in disguise: Power, beneficence, and exploitation in personal relationships. In A. Y. Lee-Chai and J. A. Bargh, *The use and abuse of power: Multiple perspectives on the causes of corruption*, 93–112. Philadelphia: Psychological Press.

Price, T. L. (2006). *Understanding ethical failures in leadership*. New York: Cambridge University Press.

Putti, J. M. (Ed.). (1991). *Management: Asian context*. Singapore: McGraw-Hill Book Co.

Putti, J. M., Koontz, H., and Weihrich, H. (1998). *Essentials of management: An Asian perspective* (5th ed.). Singapore: McGraw-Hill Book Co., in association with Singapore Institute of Management.

Pye, L. W. (1985). *Asian power and politics: The cultural dimensions of authority.* Cambridge, MA: The Belknap Press of Harvard University Press.

Rae, B. S. (2000). *Moral choices: An introduction to ethics* (2nd ed.). Grand Rapids, MI: Zondervan Publishing House.

Rappa, A. L., and Tan, S. H. (2003). Political implications of Confucian familism. *Asian Philosophy, 13* (213), 87–102.

Rardin, R. (2001). *The servant's guide to leadership: Beyond first principles.* Pittsburgh, PA: Selah Publishing.

Redding, S. G. (1993). *The spirit of Chinese capitalism.* Berlin: Walter de Gruyter & Co.

Redding, S. G., and Wong G. Y. Y. (1986). The psychology of Chinese organizational behavior. In M. H. Bond (Ed.), *The psychology of the Chinese people,* 267–95. New York: Oxford University Press.

Rest, J. R. (1986). *Moral development: Advances in research and theory.* NY: Praeger.

Rhode, D. L. (Ed.). (2006). *Moral leadership: The theory and practice of power, judgment, and policy.* San Francisco: John Wiley & Sons, Inc.

Richards, L. O, and Hoeldtke, C. (1980). *A theology of church leadership.* Grand Rapids, MI: Zondervan Publishing House.

Rickards, T., and Clark, M. (2006). *Dilemmas of leadership.* New York: Routledge.

Rinehart, S. T. (1998). *Upside down: The paradox of servant leadership.* Colorado Springs, CO: NavPress.

Rokeach, M. (1973). *The nature of human values.* New York: Free Press.

Rost, J. C. (1993). *Leadership for the 21st century.* Westport, CT: Praeger Publishing.

Rothwell, W. T. (2001). *Effective succession planning: Ensuring leadership continuity and building talent from within* (2nd ed.). New York: AMACOM.

Rush, M. D. (2002). *Management: The biblical approach.* Colorado Springs, CO: Cook Communication Ministries.

Sackmann, S. A. (2005). Responsible leadership: A cross-cultural perspective. In J. P. Doh and S. A. Stumpf (Eds.), *Handbook on responsible leadership and governance in global business,* 307–31. Northampton, MA: Edward Elgar.

Sanders, J. O. (1994). *Spiritual leadership: Principles of excellence for every believer.* Chicago: Moody Press.

Schein, E. H. (2004). The role of founder in creating organizational culture. In J. T. Wren, D. A. Hicks, and T. L. Price (Eds.), *The international library of leadership.* Cheltenham, UK: Edward Elgar Publishing Limited.

Seamands, S. (2005). *Ministry in the image of God: The Trinitarian shape of Christian service.* Downers Grove, IL: IVP Books.

Shaw, P. W. H. (2006). Vulnerable authority: A theological approach to leadership and teamwork. *Christian Education Journal,* 3, 119–33.

Shaw, W. H., and Barry, V. (1992). *Moral issues in business* (5th ed.). Belmont, CA: Wadsworth Publishing Company.

Sheh, S. W. (2003). *Chinese leadership: Moving from classical to contemporary.* Singapore: Times Media Private Limited.

Silin, R. H. (1976). *Leadership and values: The organization of large-scale Taiwanese enterprises.* Cambridge, MA: East Asian Research Center, Harvard University.

Silverthorne, C. P. (2005). *Organizational psychology in cross-cultural perspective.* New York: New York University Press.

Sison, A. J. (2006). Leadership, character and virtues from an Aristotelian viewpoint. In T. Maak and N. M. Pless (Eds.), *Responsible leadership,* 108–21. New York: Routledge.

Sledge, T. (1994). *Moving beyond your past.* Nashville, TN: Lifeway Press.

Slote, W. H. and DeVos, G. A. (Eds.). (1998). *Confucianism and the family.* New York: State University of New York Press.

Smith, B. N., Montagno, R. V., and Kuzmenko, T. N. (2004). Transformational and servant leadership: Content and contextual comparisons. *Journal of Leadership & Organizational Studies, 10* (4), 80–91.

Smith, G. (1999). *Courage and Calling: Embracing your God-given potential.* Downers Grove, IL: IVP.

Smith, P. B., and Zhong, M. W. (1996). Chinese leadership and organizational structures. In M. H. Bond (Ed.), *The handbook of Chinese psychology,* 322–37. New York: Oxford University Press.

Solomon, R. (2000). The cult, the crowd, and the community: Tensions in unity and diversity in Asian contexts. *Trinity Theological Journal,* 9, 79–96.

Soon, G. E. (Ed.). (1984). *Confucian ethics: A Christian appraisal.* Singapore: Teachers' Christian Fellowship.

Spears, L. C. (1994). Servant-leadership: Toward a new era of caring. In J. Renesch, (Ed.), *Leadership in a new era: Visionary approaches to the biggest crisis of our time,* 153–66. San Francisco: Sterling & Stone, Inc.

Spears, L. C. (Ed.). (1995). *Reflections on leadership: How Robert K. Greenleaf's theory of servant-leadership influenced today's top management thinkers.* New York: John Wiley & Sons, Inc.

Stanwick, P. A., and Stanwick, S. D. (Eds.). (2009). *Understanding business ethics* (1st ed.). Upper Saddle River, NJ: Pearson Education, Inc.

Stassen, G. H., and Gushee, D. P. (2003). *Kingdom ethics: Following Jesus in contemporary context.* Downers Grove, IL: InterVarsity Press.

Stott, J. R. W. (1978). The message of the Sermon on the Mount. In J. R. Stott (New Testament Ed.), *The Bible Speaks Today.* Leicester, UK: InterVarsity Press.

Talbert, C. H. (2004). *Reading the Sermon on the Mount: Character formation and ethical decision making in Matthew 5–7.* Grand Rapids, MI: Baker Academic.

Tan, S. Y. (2006). *Full service: Moving from self-service Christianity to total servanthood.* Grand Rapids, MI: Baker Books.

Taylor, D., and McCloskey, M. (2008, June). How to pick a President: Why virtue trumps policy. *Christianity Today,* 22–28.

Tjosvold, D., Wong, A., and Hui, C. (2004). Leadership research in Asia. In K. Leung and S. White (Eds.), *Handbook of Asian management,* 373–95. Norwell, MA: Kluwer Academic Publishers.

Tokunaga, P. (2003). *Invitation to lead: Guidance for emerging Asian American leaders.* Downers Grove, IL: IVP.

Triandis, H. C. (1995). *Individualism and collectivism.* Boulder, CO: Westview Press, Inc.

Trull, J. E., and Carter, J. E. (2004). *Ministerial ethics: Moral formation for church leaders* (2nd ed.). Grand Rapids, MI: Baker Academic.

Tseng, T. (2005). *Asian American religious leadership today: A preliminary inquiry.* Pulpit and Pew: Research on pastoral leadership. Durham, NC: Duke Divinity School.

Tu, W. M. (1985). *Confucian thought: Selfhood as creative transformation.* New York: State of University of New York Press.

Tu, W. M. (1989). *Confucianism in an historical perspective.* The Institute of East Asian Philosophies Paper and Monograph Series No. 15. Singapore: IEAP, National University of Singapore.

Vecchio, R. P. (Ed.). (1997). *Leadership: Understanding the dynamics of power and influence in organizations.* Notre Dame, IN: University of Notre Dame Press.

Waley, A. (1938). *The analects of Confucius* (English translation) New York: Random House.

Ward, T. W. (1996). Servants, leaders, and tyrants. In D. Elmer and L. McKinney (Eds.), *With an eye on the future: Development and mission in the 21st century,* 27–42. Monrovia, CA: MARC.

Watson, B. (1960). The imperial order. In W. T. De Bary, W. T. Chan, and B. Watson (Eds.), *Sources of Chinese tradition,* 174–99. New York: Columbia University Press.

Weber, M. (1947). *The theory of social and economic organizations.* (A. M. Anderson & Talcott Parsons, Trans.). New York: The Free Press.

Westwood, R. I. (Ed.) (1992). *Organisational behaviour: Southeast Asian perspectives.* Quarry Bay, Hong Kong: Longman Group (Far East) Ltd.

Westwood, R. I. (1997). Harmony and patriarchy: The cultural basis for "paternalistic headship" among overseas Chinese. *Organizational Studies, 18* (3), 445–480.

Westwood, R. I., and Chan, A. (1992). Headship and leadership. In R. I. Westwood (Ed.), *Organisational behaviour: Southeast Asian perspectives,* 118–43. Quarry Bay, Hong Kong: Longman Group (Far East) Ltd.

Westwood, R. I., and Chua, B. L. (1992). Power, politics and influence. In R. I. Westwood (Ed.), *Organisational behaviour: Southeast Asian perspectives,* 144–72. Quarry Bay, Hong Kong: Longman Group (Far East) Ltd.

Whicker, M. L. (1996). *Toxic leaders: When organizations go bad.* Wesport, CT: Quorum Books.

Whitehead, J. D., and Whitehead, E. E. (1981). *Method in ministry: Theological reflection and Christian ministry.* New York: Seabury Press.

Wilkes, C. G. (1998). *Jesus on leadership: Discovering the secrets of servant leadership from the life of Christ.* Carol Stream, IL: Tyndale House Publishers, Inc.

Wilkins, M. J. (2004). Matthew. *The NIV application commentary: from biblical text . . . to contemporary life.* Grand Rapids, MI: Zondervan.

Wingeier, D. E. (2004). Leadership: The Confucian paradigm. *Trinity Theological Journal, 12,* 121–37.

Wong, C. K. (1999). The use of natural church development to construct a strategy for equipping the English-speaking congregation at Scarborough Chinese Alliance Church. Unpublished doctoral dissertation, Fuller Theological Seminary, Pasadena, CA.

Wong, K. C. (1998). Culture and moral leadership in education. *Peabody Journal of Education, 73* (2), 106–25.

Wong, T. (2008, September 19). More China dairy products being tested. *The Straits Times,* A13.

Wright, A. F. (1964). Sui Yang-Ti: Personality and stereotype. In A. F. Wright (Ed.), *Confucianism and Chinese civilization,* 158–87. New York: Atheneum.

Wright, W. C., Jr. (2000). *Relational leadership: A biblical model for leadership service.* Carlisle, UK: Paternoster Press.

Wu, T. Y. (1987). *The Confucian way.* Singapore: Institute of East Asian Philosophies, National University of Singapore.

Yan, J. and Hunt, J. G. (2005). A cross cultural perspective on perceived leadership effectiveness. *International Journal of Cross Cultural Management, 5* (1), 49–66.

Yang, K. S. (1995). Chinese social orientation: An integrative analysis. In T. Y. Lin, W. S. Tseng, and E. K. Yeh, (Eds.) *Chinese societies and mental health*, 19–30. New York: Oxford University Press.

Yang, X. H., Peng, Y. Q., and Lee Y. T. (2008). The Confucian and Mencian philosophy of benevolent leadership. In C.C. Chen and Y. T. Lee (Eds.), *Leadership and management in China: Philosophies, theories, and practices*, 31–50. Cambridge: Cambridge University Press.

Yao, X. (2000). *Introduction to Confucianism*. Cambridge: Cambridge University Press.

Yukl, G. (2002). *Leadership in organizations* (5th ed.). Upper Saddle River, NJ: Prentice Hall.

Zaleznik, A. (1965). The dynamics of subordinacy. *Harvard Business Review*, 119–31. Boston, MA: Graduate School of Business Administration, Harvard University.

Zaleznik, A. (1977). Managers and leaders: Are they different? *Harvard Business Review* 55, (5), 67–80. Boston, MA: Graduate School of Business Administration, Harvard University.

Zaleznik, A., and Kets de Vries, M.F.R. (1975). *Power and the corporate mind*. Boston: Houghton Mifflin.

www.ingramcontent.com/pod-product-compliance
Lightning Source LLC
LaVergne TN
LVHW010938100826
845153LV00001B/81
9781498259316